Art for All

Planning for Variability in the Visual Arts Classroom

2nd Edition

LIZ BYRON LOYA

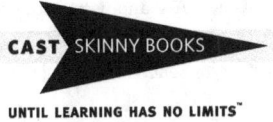

UNTIL LEARNING HAS NO LIMITS™

Bulk discounts available: For details, email publishing@cast.org or visit www.castpublishing.org

URLs used in the book may change over time. Visit the additional resources for up-to-date links at http://castpublishing.org/skinny-books/art-for-all/resources/ or email publishing@cast.org for assistance.

Copyright © 2025 by CAST, Inc.
All rights reserved.

No part of this publication may be reproduced or transmitted in any form or by any means, electronic or mechanical, including photocopy, recording, or any information storage and retrieval systems, without permission in writing from the publisher.

Library of Congress Control Number: 2024946076

Paperback ISBN 978-1-943058-28-6
Ebook ISBN 978-1-943058-29-3

Published by:
CAST Professional Publishing
an imprint of CAST, Inc.
Lynnfield, Massachusetts, USA

SKINNY BOOKS® is a registered trademark of CAST, Inc.

Cover and interior design by Happenstance Type-O-Rama

All photos are taken and copyrighted by the author except Figure 5.1, which is taken by Ms. Kat A-P and used with permission.

Cover illustration: © 2024 Seneca Loya, Cajal Loya

Contents

About the Author . . . . **v**
Acknowledgments . . . . **vii**
Introduction . . . . **vii**

1 Start With Goals **5**
   The Need for Clear Goals 9
   Key Takeaways 20

2 The Art of Engaging All Students:
   The "Why" of Instruction **21**
   Classroom Design: Messy but Organized 24
   Culturally Sustaining Pedagogy 28
   Social Emotional Learning 30
   Further Ideas for Engagement 33
   How Do You Respond to Disengagement? 36
   Designing a Highly Engaging Visual Art Lesson . . . 40
   Key Takeaways 45

3 Developing Strategic and Action-Oriented
   Learners: The "What" of Instruction **47**
   Options for Representation 51
   Experimenting With 3D Construction 55
   An Art Lesson With Multiple Means of Representation . 56
   Key Takeaways 61

4 Helping Artists Show What They Know: The "How" of Instruction 63

Options for Expression. 66
"Art Is When _____?" 70
"This Class Sucks": Welcoming All Feedback 76
An Art Lesson With Multiple Means of Action
  and Expression 77
Key Takeaways 84

5 The Burnt Banana (and Other Professional Learning Moments) . 85

The Elephant in the Room 88
"I Want to Do What I Was Doing". 92
Drinking the Water Is Not an Option. 93
Mistaken Names. 94
To Trace or Not to Trace?. 95
Making UDL Implementation Sustainable 97
A Word about Cell Phones 99
A Final Note 104
Key Takeaways 106

References **107**
Additional Reading **111**

About the Author

Liz Byron Loya is a practicing artist and the K–8 visual art teacher at Mildred Avenue K–8, a Boston (MA) public school. Liz is a Massachusetts professionally licensed teacher in visual art, special education, ESL, middle school math, and elementary education. During her career, she has taught almost every subject, working with students from preschool through graduate school.

Liz earned her bachelor's degree in Studio Art and Elementary Education from Boston College. She received a master's in Arts in Education from the Harvard Graduate School of Education and an MEd in Special Education (moderate disabilities) from Lesley University.

She has presented on Universal Design for Learning (UDL) internationally and been a featured keynote speaker at various education conferences. She is a CAST National Faculty member and leads various education professional development workshops and courses on UDL. Liz is continually working to enhance her instruction by applying UDL and is perpetually inspired by her students and the arts.

Acknowledgments

Pen to paper, fingers to keys, publish, print, show them
dyslexic writing, while wanting what Whitman yearned,
my "very flesh shall be a great poem…"
so *you*, go now "re-examine all" you learned…
you the reader, first appreciated in this list
written with *you* at the center, educator, colleague, the artist
the student, all of us, always students.

Built with many hearts and hands
Strong leaders, eternal respect for yeses and not yets
with gratitude GPA art was planned
Parent Council, art lovers, reviews of budgets
Thank you to the families, guardians, parents,
teaching a greatest joy and learning process,
students: my purpose transparent.
Debbie O'Shea: managing middle school looks effortless
every day. Dearest friend, best teacher inherent.

Thanks to the makers of Grammarly
CAST's cast of dedicated educators
WPS teachers in the Art of Variability
You: inspiration and UDL creators
while composing this little tome, unexpected experience
Dr. Jenna C., your unmatched compassion and honesty
anchored me, no moral lassitude or variance
Sheila, your skill, our meetings, guiding attitude
thanks to all, this was composed
and the third to last word, life's composed.

If you know, thank you for sharing yours,
you're my bookends,
love opens doors.

Caroline, anchor, sisterhood-best friend defined,
Tom, Elise, nieces, nephews, in-laws and more
Support, secure, memories created and on rewind
Family is forever, for this I am grateful for.
With gratitude and appreciation
to a Greater Being above
Genetics, Eternal Education, *thanks Mom and Dad,*
Always all my love

Best second edition additions,
Carlos, Seneca, y Cajal
My loves, purpose, mission—
You're my center, core, and all.

Introduction

I've always been fascinated by the concept of time. It can both race by and drag on, with a lot unfolding in a brief period, while very little may change over an extended duration. Our engagement and emotions heavily influence our perception of time, as it can feel fleeting when we're absorbed in something and, conversely, slow when we are facing challenges.

Since I wrote the first edition of *Art for All*, the world has experienced a global pandemic, a significant reckoning with race, and the impact of artificial intelligence, all of which have had consequential shifts in education and, at times, made me feel like days were dragging on or flying by. Personally, I have undergone substantial growth and learning in these years, leading to some gaps in this book.

Since the first edition, I've embraced new roles as a spouse and a mother, had my job cut, found a new art teaching position, and been honored to speak with and teach thousands of educators about UDL. The UDL Guidelines have also been extensively reviewed and revised to be more inclusive and to address systemic barriers. These updates to the guidelines, personal transformations, and larger global shifts have also influenced my approach to instruction and UDL.

Approximately four months after publishing *Art for All*, my school, Gardner Pilot Academy (GPA), decided to cut the visual art teaching position due to a limited budget. So for all you art teachers who've experienced job insecurity…I'm right there with you! I could have stayed at GPA and returned to teach special education, ESL, or math, but my heart is with art. Therefore I decided to continue to teach art and feel immense gratitude to be teaching at Mildred Avenue K–8, another Boston Public School with a thriving arts department.

Transitioning to a new school revitalized my teaching. The transition also brought to the forefront of my pedagogy how vastly different school cultures are and how school culture impacts teaching and learning. The transition required that I dramatically shift my instruction and classroom management to meet the needs of a completely different demographic of students. It only reinforced the core foundation of UDL, that our curriculum design cannot just be retrofitted with UDL but must be designed from the beginning with clear, flexible, rigorous goals. Teaching in a different school reaffirmed that learner variability is as unique as one's fingerprint and that UDL isn't a curriculum in a box.

My transition to a new school also developed my understanding of where barriers to learning can be. My greatest "aha" has been that the educator can sometimes be a barrier to student learning, and since then, I have been on a mission to improve how my presence in the classroom impacts learning. This second edition also highlights how UDL is connected to Culturally Sustaining Pedagogy (CSP) and Social Emotional Learning (SEL). These concepts have been implicit but not explicit in the UDL Guidelines until the latest version (3.0) was released in 2024. See https://udlguidelines.cast.org for more information.

• • •

Since publishing *Art for All*, I have had the privilege and honor of presenting on UDL and the arts in workshops, graduate classes, and conferences across the world. I often get asked a variety of questions, two of which I'd like to address here. First, people ask, "How do you suggest I start implementing UDL? Or if someone is new to UDL, how do they get started implementing it?"

My answer: start small, with manageable changes to your physical classroom and/or curriculum. If you try to do too much, you might start with a bang but realize it isn't sustainable because it feels like more work, and then your attempt at implementing UDL will fail. Incorporating UDL into your daily practice is truly like rolling a snowball: your skills and knowledge will gradually grow and build upon each other one day at a time. I'm still rolling my snowball 20 years after beginning to learn about UDL.

If you are brand new to UDL or know a teacher who is new to it, I suggest you first evaluate your physical classroom space. Where are the barriers? What can you change so that students have better access to materials or information? I love making changes to the physical space because it's something you do once and you don't have to constantly revisit. Then consider your instruction: Where are the biggest barriers that are related to engagement, representation, or action and expression? Pick one principle and design one or two changes to a unit of study that are going to proactively reduce or remove *one* barrier. Ask your students what they think and note if there was an impact.

Incorporate reflective practice into your daily routine, in which you question and consider how your personal experiences and/or biases impact student learning.

Continue to learn about your students to ensure you are designing instruction for them. Gradually push yourself out of your comfort zone.

Another common question I field is "How is designing art instruction with UDL different from choice-based art classes?" While there is an overlap between UDL and choice-based instruction, there are significant differences when you consider what each of these instructional frameworks involves.

Choice-based art education emphasizes student autonomy and decision-making in the artistic process, allowing students to choose their projects, materials, techniques, and themes. UDL may, at times, include choice, but it also encompasses many other aspects of learning in a visual art classroom. UDL focuses on clear, rigorous, and flexible learning goals with multiple means of representation for students to understand content. It also supports student autonomy, decision-making, self-regulation, and goal setting while providing options for self-assessment and methods for designing physical classroom space.

While choice-based art instruction can be aligned with UDL principles, it is important to note that choice-based instruction alone is not universally designed simply because it offers choice. UDL goes beyond choice to ensure equal opportunities for all students to learn by providing various means of representation, action, and engagement tailored to individual needs.

1

Start With Goals

In 2007, I was first introduced to Universal Design for Learning (UDL) in a namesake course at the Harvard Graduate School of Education while earning a master's in Arts in Education. David Rose, the "father" of UDL himself,

Figure 1.1. Kindergarteners present their visual art portfolios.

taught the course. I was fresh out of undergrad and had only four semesters of student teaching under my belt. UDL seemed to be a repackaged method for "good teaching." I resisted the thought that this "framework" was a neoteric way of thinking about teaching and learning. Needless to say, I earned a B+ in the course, and let's be honest, taking into account grade inflation, a B+ is more like a D in graduate school.

Each year since then, I have grown from resisting UDL to accepting it to implementing it into every lesson. While I spent seven years teaching special education, English as a second language, and middle-school math, my passion had always been in the arts. In 2016, I was offered my dream job. My school—Gardner Pilot Academy—created a full-time visual art teaching position and I transitioned to the role.

I was ecstatic. I would finally get to use my undergraduate degree in Studio Art and a master's in Arts in Education in combination with my special education experience. I would design and implement arts instruction using the UDL framework that I had spent the past ten years learning, practicing, and teaching to my peers. I would do so in a challenging but also highly supportive environment. Gardner Pilot Academy is a full-inclusion, preK–8 public school in Boston, Massachusetts. As a full-inclusion school, we teach many students with disabilities in the general classroom who would otherwise be placed in a separate setting. In addition, more than 80% of Gardner's 400 students are identified as "high need." Most live far below the poverty line, and many have directly experienced or witnessed trauma. A majority are English language learners and a quarter of students have an identified disability.

This book shares what I've learned about using UDL to teach the visual arts. To get the most out of this book, you should already have a fundamental knowledge of Universal Design for Learning. You know that UDL is a framework for teaching in which the curriculum and environment are designed to reduce barriers by providing learners with multiple options or means for engagement, representation, and action and expression (CAST, 2024). Those principles are expanded upon with Guidelines and checkpoints that show ways to reduce barriers and increase support so all learners can reach their potential. This book does not cover the basics of UDL. Rather we look at how to implement UDL in the visual arts classroom.

> **PAUSE AND THINK** Reflect on your knowledge of UDL. Do you know enough of the UDL basics or would it be helpful to review the guidelines and other foundational material first? Read the UDL Guidelines at http://udlguidelines.cast.org.

If you're reading this, you also likely understand how the arts teach specific habits that uniquely contribute to expert learning. Hetland et al. (2013) identify and describe the many "habits of mind" students experience when working in the arts. These include the ability to develop craft, engage and persist, envision, express, observe, reflect, stretch and explore, and understand art worlds. Arts educator and author Lisa Philips (2013) has found that the skills students glean from the arts not only support students developing into artists but contribute to them developing into leaders and creative thinkers. These skills include perseverance, accountability, responding to constructive feedback, and non-verbal communications skills.

These skills, or "habits of mind," dovetail with the UDL framework, which emphasizes helping students become learners who are resourceful, engaged, and strategic. Such learners can formulate personal learning goals, self-regulation strategies, and know what resources they need to learn as well as how they can most successfully express what they know (Meyer et al., 2014). Later chapters of this book will explicitly examine these qualities in relationship to each of the three principles.

As art educators, we know how challenging it is at times to have our work recognized, validated, and adequately funded. This should make us more empathetic to those students who feel marginalized in school, including our art classrooms—those who face barriers both in the curriculum and the environment. Students who typically struggle to be engaged in art or who do not present "grade-level" skills can fully participate in visual art when instruction and the environment are universally designed. On the flip side of the spectrum, there are always some if not several students who present visual creations that far exceed developmental expectations. Our most prolific and creative thinkers, however, can be stifled when instruction is wedded to a narrow goal or specific outcome. Fortunately, UDL is designed to provide students in the margins with deeper, more effective access to learning.

 SMART TIP Try using Novak and Rodriguez's "UDL Progression Rubric" (2018) to assess your own UDL competencies and set professional practice goals that directly align with the UDL Guidelines. Visit http://castpublishing.org/skinny-books/art-for-all/resources/.

www.ingramcontent.com/pod-product-compliance
Lightning Source LLC
Chambersburg PA
CBHW070113080526
44586CB00013B/1285

In many cases, visual art teachers are among the few educators in a school who work with every child. This is a special opportunity to immerse large numbers of students in content and an environment that is accessible and inspiring. It is, however, challenging to adequately support such a large number of students who do not have frequent enough classes to quickly build teacher-student relationships or practice routines. In addition, in the case of my school, most of our "core" subjects have additional staff in the room to support our inclusion model. Very rarely do art classes receive the same support. Adding to the challenge, many art educators provide instruction to students who take our classes as a required "special," not as an elective. These students do not enthusiastically enter the art room ready to learn and create. The young artist in the margins requires a curriculum free of barriers to realize their innate artistic skills. Inspiration and creativity thrive when the individual feels they can access the content. Art educators, however, are not helpless. We cannot use our work conditions as excuses for not quite reaching all students.

Using the principles of UDL can help us plan for all learners as we recognize that "disability" and "inaccessibility" are characteristics of the curriculum and the environment, not the person. Through this lens, teaching a wide range of learners becomes feasible. It may be beneficial to have multiple licenses or certifications to teach special populations, but if you become well-versed in UDL, you will be able to systematically design and deliver instruction for all.

The Need for Clear Goals

In art instruction, as in any other subject, creating an inclusive and effective learning environment doesn't happen through good intentions or talking a great game. It happens by design, and design begins with a vision of the outcome. What are our goals for a unit or a lesson? What do we want our art instruction to accomplish?

In planning art instruction, educators may be tempted to start by considering means and methods. How do we make something? What materials do we use? Universal Design for Learning encourages us to start our planning with the learning goals, leaving the means and materials for accomplishing that goal open. The means are the specific ways students accomplish the goal, such as drawing, painting, or writing. An example of a universally designed visual art goal without definitive means is: "Students will create a monochromatic image." The verb *create* is general and opens your planning to more options for showing monochromatic images. There's not necessarily one way to do this.

Establishing clear instructional and learning goals is the foundation for the rest of your UDL planning (Meyer et al., 2014). Goals should, if possible, be written in a way that allows flexibility in the means and materials used to achieve them. For example, a goal that states "Students will create different colors by combining the primary colors" gives students more options for learning about color theory because the goal is clear yet broad enough to incorporate multiple means. Access to art evolves to inclusion when there are multiple paths for expression. In this assignment, students can:

- Mix paint with a variety of tools.
- Select the degree of challenge by subdividing their paper into many or few sections for each new color.
- Choose a sheet of paper with pre-drawn subdivisions as an option.
- Choose how and where to place paint.

- Determine their own proportions of each color in a designated section.
- Synthesize their understanding of color theory in multiple ways (discuss, show, write, present, annotate).

By contrast, the same goal could be written as: *Students will create the colors needed for a color wheel using a template or worksheet*. This goal would require students to follow a step-by-step procedure to reach the goal. Students would need to be able to read a worksheet and would not be able to vary the demands of the lesson. This goal is more limiting and would likely result in a lesson fraught with barriers.

Sometimes lesson goals *do* focus on a particular skill—drawing, for example, or sculpting. There may still be flexibility in the means and materials. When a goal incorporates the means—for example, "Students will paint a monochromatic image using the value scale and tempera paint"—ensure you have planned options to support the means. Students could have flexibility in choosing the subject of their painting, the scale of their paper, the color, or an artist or work of art to transform into a monochromatic work.

UDL goals keep expectations high for all students by focusing the rigor of the instruction on meaningful lessons accompanied by multiple opportunities for them to be engaged and express their understanding.

SMART TIP Google and use Bloom's Taxonomy of Action Verbs or Hess's Cognitive Rigor Matrix to help you locate appropriate verbs for the "means" of your goals.

As students begin to internalize the flexibility of the means within a lesson, they sometimes begin to ask some version of the question, "Can I do something else?" I then inquire, "What is it you want to do?" If their idea relates to the goal and we have the materials, then I fully support their ambition.

If their idea does not relate to the goal, I redirect them according to the expectations. I work with students to determine if the idea can be reformulated to connect to the goal. Depending on the unit and length of the lesson, I sometimes tell students that once they demonstrate the goal, then they can work on the other idea. Art class does not and cannot become a "Choose your own adventure"; if you start your planning with a clear goal, your instruction will be more focused, and the goal will bolster your response to student requests.

UDL is not a curriculum in a box; goal writing is not formulaic. However, here are some touchpoints to help keep you on track.

- Your goals should
    - focus your planning and instruction,
    - support the variability of learners with multiple means for each of the three UDL principles, and
    - align with a state or national visual art standard.
- The means of your goal should
    - align with the purpose of the lesson, and
    - reduce barriers by providing construct-relevant methods, materials, and assessments.

After identifying potential barriers to learning, crafting a clear goal with flexible means is critical to designing a fully inclusive art lesson. A clear goal directs your planning, while the flexible means allow you to consider options that engage and challenge both your most skilled and innately creative students as well as your students who do not identify as artists.

In one of my early childhood lessons, the goal "I can use and describe lines in my art" was flexible enough to provide meaningful and rigorous options for all students. Some students used rulers to draw and name vertical, diagonal, and horizontal lines while examining works by Wassily Kandinsky, Joan Miro, Kenesha Sneed, and Piet Mondrian. These students went on to create developmentally complex and often precise pieces. Other students were beginning to learn correct pencil grip. They began by finding and pointing to lines in works of art or the classroom. These students had the option of using a ruler and drawing tools but could create freehand linear works or place pre-cut squares in a line. All students were presented with all options, giving everyone the opportunity to explore their learning threshold. A clear and flexible goal also contributed to more authentic and individualized assessment without the need to create multiple activities and rubrics.

If the goal of the lesson had been historically predictable, it might have read: *Students will use crayons to draw three types of lines by using a ruler to make art similar to Mondrian.* With a narrower goal, the lesson would be planned with inherent barriers. The assessment of the goal would be unnecessarily confining and those students in the margins either would not be able to access the art-making process or would have their advanced abilities stifled. With such a means-specific and narrow goal, student art will inevitably look like cookie-cutter art, and when all your students produce very similar-looking pieces, not only are you depriving them of their creative expression, but it's also a sign you aren't designing with UDL.

PAUSE AND THINK

1. What is a universally designed goal?
2. How does UDL help us think about methods and materials?

Using Goals to Measure Student Growth

A clear goal sets the stage for authentic formative and summative assessments. A formative assessment is any assessment that occurs during instruction, allowing students to self-monitor their progress and providing the teacher with information to adjust instruction. Summative assessments take place at the conclusion of a unit or lesson and often occur less frequently.

An assessment begins with an observation followed by some form of documentation or recording. This aspect can be challenging for the art teacher, who may see hundreds of students per week. Be strategic and selective with your assessments to avoid burnout. Have students actively participate in the assessment process to increase engagement and provide options for motivation and goal setting. After documenting, analyze the assessments and then communicate the outcomes. The analysis of the assessment can also incorporate student voice, providing options to enhance capacity for monitoring progress.

 A CLOSER LOOK Explore the National Core Arts Standards Model Cornerstone Assessments at https://tinyurl.com/VisualMCA.

UDL WITHIN VISUAL ART PEDAGOGIES

Many art educators are probably familiar with choice-based art instruction that often falls under the pedagogy of TAB: Teaching for Artistic Behaviors. TAB is a methodology in which the educator sets up several art-making options and allows students to select their center or station. Each station gives students the freedom to create while the teacher responds to the students' interests (Douglas & Jaquith, 2009).

The challenge with TAB is that it often lacks a central goal. Students can produce without inhibition, but unless they are already engaged learners (motivated and purposeful), they can create art almost aimlessly. In addition, measuring learning is more difficult when the goal is unclear. However, when planned with the UDL Guidelines in mind, TAB can provide students with clear goals while also giving multiple options for action and expression, engagement, and representation.

Similarly, *Studio Thinking 2* (Hetland et al., 2013) is an excellent framework for providing multiple options in art instruction and teaching creative "habits of mind." Planning a lesson based solely on the structures and habits of mind could potentially create barriers for students. For example, a teacher might implement the studio habit of "Develop Craft: Technique, Studio Practice" by providing students with clean-up roles as part of a routine (2013, p. 44). Without UDL, however, implicit barriers for students go unaddressed. The lesson might not be relevant to students: Why should they care if the classroom space is clean? The demo or lecture component of representing the content might be inaccessible for some learners: What if a student cannot follow multi-step oral directions, or the student might perform tasks more consistently with the options of a visual checklist? What if

(continues)

(continued)

students have a preference for a specific role based on prior experiences? With UDL the teacher would plan multiple means for supporting students' understanding of classroom community and engaging in a task that sometimes doesn't seem as thrilling as the artmaking itself.

A teacher interviewed in *Studio Thinking 2* notes how messy Alexander Calder's space was but says that because he worked alone, his disorganization did not affect anyone. What if she planned a visual of his studio next to an image of the classroom full of students, and then expanded that image to include the dozens of classes that rotate through the space on a weekly basis? To represent the clean-up process, she could not only orally state directions and do quick demonstrations, but also show a 1-to-2-minute student-made film of students from the school showing clean-up routines. I have done this in my classroom and used the videos year after year. She could allow students to choose their clean-up task instead of delineating it. The clean-up jobs could also be represented with visual "clean-up job" passes attached to a color-coded lanyard.

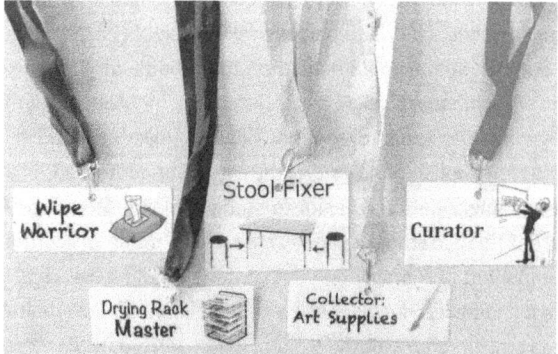

Figure 1.2. Color-coded clean-up passes not only make the routine more efficient, but also give students a role to play.

> *(continued)*
>
> *Studio Thinking 2* is brimming with examples of visual art teachers presenting powerful lessons to variable students. If your planning and instruction stop there, then you could potentially miss the students in the margins. The objectives of each lesson are clear, but the flexibility in lesson design is sometimes limiting. Each exemplar has elements of UDL, but without naming barriers, explicitly understanding the guidelines, and planning with them, the studio habits of mind and studio structures are not enough to captivate all audiences.
>
> Regardless of the visual art methodology or pedagogy you use, planning with UDL is imperative to meeting all your students' needs. UDL is essential for some learners but powerful for all, as everyone in the class benefits from exposure to various options for expressing a goal.

For example, in one of my classes, the unit goal states, "Students will have one well-made 3D vessel." Students know what they need to create, but they also have multiple means for doing so and measuring their performance. We extensively discuss what "well-made" means, and the reality is that this descriptor looks different depending on the piece and the artist. Students are assessed using either a collaboratively created rubric, an independently made rubric, or a rubric I provide. I give students the criteria for success at the onset of the unit and provide opportunities for them to self-reflect throughout class. I evaluate their comprehension of key vocabulary through exit tickets and "do nows" that challenge students to recall and explain vocabulary in authentic ways. They are given formative assessments in the form of reflection exercises where they select an aspect of their piece that meets the criteria and an aspect that they feel they can improve. Students are asked to articulate how they would enhance their piece either aesthetically or structurally. They can choose one of several characteristics of 3D art that are provided in a word bank if they need additional support using content-specific language. Students engage in quick peer critiques, where they evaluate a classmate's piece. They also articulate the goal, and the steps they take to achieve the goal, as another option for interacting with the content. In the end, the assessments not only measure but also enhance learning.

The National Core Arts Standards offer several grade-specific Model Cornerstone Assessments (MCAs). Each MCA includes examples of summative and formative assessments throughout a unit. Examples of student artwork serve as benchmarks for the standards taught in each unit. Each MCA provides detailed assessment procedures, rubrics, student self-reflection forms, and strategies for embedding assessment into instruction. While each MCA only represents a fraction of the content you might teach, the methods for assessment are easily transferable to other lessons and grade levels.

SMART TIP When co-creating a rubric with your class, start by having them describe the qualities of a highly successful piece, then scaffold the description down from there. The more students are engaged in their own assessment, the more efficient and reliable their assessments will become.

In any class, there are always a few students who try to challenge a goal and its assessment by doing the least amount of work possible. However, since most students in a universally designed class are deeply engaged, I am freed up to have a 1:1 or small-group discussion with those students who are not reaching for high standards. In these conversations, we discuss the goal and what barriers they are facing to push themselves out of their comfort zone. When I have not designed instruction with a clear goal and flexible means, I have many more students who attempt to do the minimum or are so disengaged and unaccountable that they often present inappropriate school behaviors or an apathetic disposition.

The goal is the starting place for implementing UDL. You can picture it as the first vertex of a triangle. It is the piece you will use to align all your planning, instruction, and assessment. From your goal, you plot the second point by determining what will be instructionally different because you are planning with UDL. The student learning outcome is the third point. After this point you compose a new goal, reflecting on components of UDL that were successful with students and areas that still present learning barriers. As you cycle back, the process becomes iterative and leads to continual professional growth, as each time you plan with a clear goal, you drive your instruction toward fewer and fewer barriers.

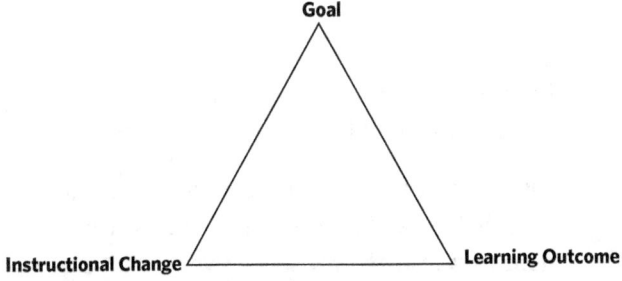

Without the goal, your lesson lacks direction and the starting point is missing. So take the time up front to work on—to really *design*—your unit or lesson goals and the accompanying assessments. Doing so will help keep you and your students focused on growing as learners and artists.

PAUSE AND THINK

1. How can you incorporate UDL goals and design instruction within your current curriculum and pedagogy?

2. How are you planning to measure these goals?

A CLOSER LOOK Check out the VSA/Kennedy Center's Visual Art Teacher Resource Guide, which includes eight UDL visual art lesson plans for grades K–12. See https://tinyurl.com/VSAKennedyTRG.

Key Takeaways

- Universally designed goals and assessments keep you focused on learning objectives. Methods and materials become a means to that end.

- Visual art teachers can create authentic and reliable forms of assessment to measure student growth in a highly subjective content area.

- UDL can revolutionize your instruction by providing all students with options for excelling in art.

2

The Art of Engaging All Students: The "Why" of Instruction

In general, an engaged learner is purposeful and motivated, but what characterizes a purposeful and motivated learner in the visual art classroom?

Figure 2.1. Seventh graders engaged in monochromatic painting

Early childhood art teachers know that "engagement"—colloquially defined as "wanting to do something"—is rarely the primary barrier for their students. Young artists typically enter the art classroom with enthusiasm and motivation to learn, marked by an egocentric infallibility. They need options for understanding the goal of the lesson, naming basic steps to achieve the goal, and following through with those steps. Examples of these choices could include using multiple means to present the goal of the lesson. I have had students sing the goal, make motions to represent the goal, and explain the goal in their own words. I only have students read the goal with me once, as reading fluency and decoding skills are not skills directly needed to attain the goal in most art lessons.

Depending on whether a student is participating in art as a required class or as an elective impacts engagement. Students in late elementary and middle school who are required to take art have likely already self-identified as either an artist or non-artist based on the perceptions of their abilities. Those who do not see themselves as artists or do not perceive the value in learning art will encounter curricular barriers if multiple options are not embedded. The students who employ a growth mindset demonstrate engagement, especially at this developmental stage (Dweck, 2006). Moreover, such learners demonstrate coping strategies for overcoming frustrations with difficult tasks, creative blocks, or unexpected emotional reactions. They independently direct energy to thoughtful reflection on their emotions and use those ideas to stimulate their artistic growth.

Most high school students who engage in art are taking the class as an elective, but if students are to develop into learners who are purposeful and reflective, multiple means for engagement can help them increase stamina and persistence. Engagement at this level might include students developing personalized artistic goals, forms of assessment, and timelines for project completion. Engaged artists at the high school level have usually internalized behaviors and strategies to support purposeful work and motivation, even when faced with challenging tasks. Regardless of the developmental stage of your artists, you must optimize and adjust the right kind of choice and the level of independence to ensure engagement (CAST, 2018).

As art teachers, not only do we typically teach dozens of students per week, but we observe vastly different classroom behaviors. When a student is struggling with the content or behavior, remind yourself that the barrier is in the content, curriculum, and/or environment, or may even be embedded in you as the teacher, due to your unconscious bias—the barriers are not within the student. If you are engaged in a task, you are much less likely to be distracted, defiant, disruptive, or physically or emotionally unsafe. Consider options to remove the barrier and make sure they relate to the goal of the lesson.

In my experience, the engagement principle can be challenging to implement if I have a weak or uninformed relationship with a student. Teachers who make art experiences relevant to their students also make personal connections with students; these connections can correlate to fewer behavioral conflicts. At times, this might require teachers to stretch their preferences, as good teaching is sometimes great acting. Consider yourself a salesperson for art, and your job is to make the lesson so enticing that everyone in your audience will want to buy into it.

On other occasions, what is best for the student may not always be what feels comfortable for the teacher. For example, students who need to fidget to focus may distract teachers, causing them to ask students to remain still during instruction. Teachers' inflexibility can be an instructional or behavioral barrier if what the students need to perform is actually an appropriate option for learning. For those in the margins, the UDL principle of engagement can build student-teacher relationships and an inclusive environment, which directly influence performance and learning in the arts.

> **PAUSE AND THINK**
>
> 1. What characterizes a purposeful and motivated expert artist in your classroom?
>
> 2. How can you use UDL to help build stronger relationships with students?

Classroom Design: Messy but Organized

Let's start with classroom design, because creating an engaging space is an important first step in designing an engaging visual arts curriculum. While all the UDL Guidelines have components that influence your classroom environment, most checkpoints specifically relating to the environment fall within the engagement category.

Visual art classrooms or carts can quickly become disorganized and overstimulating due to the variety of art supplies used on a daily basis as well as the amount of student work created. Regularly used art supplies should be accessible to all students and labeled with a visual cue and text. You could even consider fastening an example of the actual supply to the front of a bin. Not only does this strategy remove the barrier of reading, but it also allows students with visual impairments to feel the object. In my classroom, all basic supplies are available to all students because they are on a low enough shelf for everyone to access. All supply bins have an image of the items with a Spanish and an English label. The labels are laminated and hot-glued to the bins to increase the longevity of the system. If you have supply bins in the middle of your classroom's tables and you often find the supplies misplaced, consider taking a photo of a well-organized bin and placing the photo in the center of the bin. Then during the clean-up transition, remind students to make sure the containers look like the photos. If you don't have a dedicated classroom and instead use a cart, you can apply the same strategy by taking a photo of your organized cart and remind students that the cart should mirror the photo.

Figure 2.2. All supply bins have an image of the items with a Spanish and an English label.

Figure 2.3. Kindergarten students demonstrate some of the steps to cleaning up. I use slides similar to these images for every clean-up routine.

You can further remove transitional barriers and develop students' executive functioning by breaking down multi-step clean-up processes. Consider using photos of your students completing each step of the clean-up transition. These images could be projected or printed on an anchor chart, making the complex task more engaging and accessible to more students than checklists or relying only on verbal directions. Similar strategies can be used for an art cart. Depending on the needs of your students and your classroom management, you could give students autonomy over retrieving and returning supplies. Younger students often need defined roles when being asked to transition to clean-up. Removing complete autonomy does not mean you are not incorporating UDL; be sensitive to the developmental needs of your students and what is manageable within your skill set as an instructor. Art is messy, but it does not have to be disorganized.

Art supplies that either cost more or are dangerous are not readily available to students. Knowing where these items are located, however, is crucial to students' creativity. When students ask for an X-Acto knife, tacks, Velcro, tiles, or a hot-glue gun, creating is more efficient if the teacher can immediately retrieve the item. This interaction can also stimulate the teacher to ask the student how their idea connects with the goal.

You can re-envision your physical classroom design or art cart to make learning more accessible for all. Consider having tables of various heights and a range of seating options. A space in your room with cushions or pillows provides further choices for seating. If possible, create nooks for individuals who work better with fewer distractions. The lighting in your room can also have a positive effect on affect if it is warm and dispersed. Many classrooms are outfitted with panels of fluorescent lights, which are not conducive to creating a calming environment. If you have your own classroom, consider using ambient light or lamp light. Yard sales, church sales, and thrift shops often have many low-cost options for lighting. The same is true for finding alternative seating and tables. If you are an "Art on a Cart" teacher who pushes into other teachers' rooms, you have fewer opportunities to alter the space, but you can still allow students to have options for flexible seating and grouping.

Figure 2.4. A space in your room for cushions or pillows provides further choices for seating.

> **A CLOSER LOOK** Visit http://castpublishing.org/skinny-books/art-for-all/resources/ to see images of UDL classroom environments (including before photos, after photos, and photos that show the evolution of the space and walls over time), classroom labels, and student job labels that can be printed out and used.

Culturally Sustaining Pedagogy

As you think about student engagement, take care to consider the principles of Culturally Sustaining Pedagogy

(CSP). CSP is an instructional approach that aims to support and maintain the cultural and linguistic identities of students, families, and communities. This approach has always been implicit in UDL but with Guidelines 3.0, CSP is more plainly spelled out as they call for "welcoming interests and identities" (engagement), designing options that "represent a diversity of perspectives and identities in authentic ways" (representation), and addressing "biases related to modes of expression and communication" (action and expression). CSP calls on educators not only to acknowledge and affirm students' cultural backgrounds but also to actively sustain and integrate them into the learning process. CSP promotes equity across racial and ethnic communities and values community languages and practices. It is a dynamic approach that recognizes culture as a set of often complex values, beliefs, and practices that vary across students' identities (California Department of Education, 2023; Chajed, 2024; Institute of Education Sciences, 2024).

When I reflected on how I incorporated CSP into my UDL instruction, I initially made sure that my students could see themselves in the curriculum through examples of artists and artworks that they could relate to culturally, racially, or socially. This didn't mean I never exposed them to artists who are dramatically different from them; it just meant including them in the curriculum was a priority. Upon switching schools, I had to completely upend much of my content because the demographic of my student body had changed entirely.

Another aspect of CSP I focused on at the onset was to create clear lines of communication between home and school that worked for families. But to fully implement CSP on a less superficial level, I needed to make my students feel comfortable to question and challenge the instruction, and I realized they were not going to do this unless my relationships with them were strengthened and more authentic. Truly taking my practice to the next level and more fully implementing CSP with UDL meant I had to unpack the previously unidentified barrier in the classroom, which was me. My assumptions and implicit biases could derail a thoughtfully designed UDL lesson. I was and am sometimes the barrier to engagement. Check out chapter 5 to read more on CSP.

Social Emotional Learning

In recent years, Social Emotional Learning (SEL) has also moved to the forefront of the curriculum. Incorporating SEL into your instruction can be achieved in various ways. One simple and authentic way I incorporate SEL is by explicitly telling students, particularly those in grades 4–8, that my goal as their teacher is for them to learn and love art, but first and foremost, I want the class to be "fun and chill." The words *fun* and *chill* are chosen for their simplicity and developmental relatability. Students can't learn or enjoy art in a heightened emotional state, and it's essential for them to be aware of this goal and regularly assess the classroom climate (Heissel & Norris, 2019).

At the conclusion of most classes, I do a quick check-in by asking students to give a thumbs up if the class was "fun" and another thumbs up if it was "chill." Based on the responses, we have a quick check-in to discuss what went well and what could be improved. I also always have an anonymous comment box for students to use as an option for participation. I openly welcome feedback for improving the class and let students know what actionable steps I will take to address concerns. Consistently asking these check-in questions at the end of class reminds students that you are continually striving to create an environment where they can thrive. Plus students appreciate that having fun and learning in a relaxed (chill) environment is something I openly value.

Think about how you want your students to feel during class and what emotional state you learn best in. Ask your students the same questions. Your end-of-class check-in will likely look and feel different, using different language or gathering responses in a different format. However, it's essential to incorporate some consistent and efficient way to gauge students' social and emotional states during class to identify and reduce barriers to learning that you might not even be aware of.

Ever since I began teaching, I'd occasionally find myself in moments of silent frustration because it seemed like my students had no idea how much time I had put into planning lessons or had any inkling of how much I cared about them. Firstly, this response isn't helpful, taking things personally, expecting students to jump for joy at a lesson, and/or feeling like a martyr for all your work doesn't produce better learning outcomes. But soon after publishing *Art for All*, I had an "aha" moment. I reflected on the concept of "caring" and the ways that a teacher and students can demonstrate caring. I likened these ways to *The 5 Love Languages*, a well-known book by Gary Chapman (2010), who outlines five ways a romantic partner can demonstrate and receive love. My metaphor for my students used a similar approach, minus any romance, of course. I discussed with my students five ways they could receive and show caring in the classroom and asked them what their preference was for both receiving caring and showing they care.

These are the five ways:

- Words of affirmation: Saying publicly or privately how you are cared for.
- Appropriate physical touch: Giving a high five, secret handshake, pat on the back, or side hug.
- Acts of service: Going out of your way to help a student with a project or with clean-up.
- "Gifts": Giving stickers, small toys, or items from a rewards box.
- Quality time: Setting aside special lunch in the art room, or allowing extra art time before or after school or during recess (sometimes, with the classroom teacher's agreement, students can spend 30 minutes on a Friday in my class getting extra art instead of regular instruction).

Prior to outlining the five "languages" of caring in the classroom, I had been primarily showing my students I cared through my devotion to planning engaging lessons, and they had no idea that was my best way to show I cared. My frustration wasn't because my students were ungrateful, it was because I was basing my reaction on an assumption. After discussing the five languages of caring in the classroom, most students said they prefer words of affirmation, so I made sure to sincerely start and end class by literally telling them I care about them and sharing explicit, goal-based shout-outs. Wow, what a difference that made—it strengthened my relationships with all my students. There were also students who surprised me by requesting that I show them I care through one of the other languages, and with that knowledge, I was able to tailor my approach with them.

Students also realized that they had a preference for how they showed they cared about someone, and many had never realized that they could show caring in another way. We took the time to discuss examples of each of the five languages of caring in the classroom and intentionally practiced each to see which felt the most natural to us.

With all this said, I thought I was onto something big, and that there should be a book about these five languages of caring. I googled the idea, and to my surprise, Chapman already had written a book titled *5 Love Languages for Children* (as well as books on five love languages for the workplace, for apologies, and for the military). Regardless of whether you read his book or not, think about how you naturally prefer to show you care for your students and what barriers that might inadvertently create. Consider discussing with your students the five languages as an SEL strategy and be sure to provide options for representation (anchor charts, act it out, verbally explain). The beauty is that these languages can be used organically on a daily basis to strengthen your classroom climate and reduce barriers to communicating caring.

Further Ideas for Engagement

UDL is a framework for teaching and does not fit neatly in a textbook or a teacher's guide, though I know teachers crave practical examples of UDL in action. As you read the following potential strategies for engagement, keep in mind that these are only a fraction of the possible means for engagement (visit http://castpublishing.org/skinny-books/art-for-all/resources/ for more ideas). The most powerful options evolve with the specific barriers students face.

Example 1: Options for Self-Regulation, Self-Assessment, and Reflection (Emotional Capacity)

Key questions

Do you have students create criteria for effective art critiques? Do you provide options for students to reflect on and evaluate their feelings and behaviors?

Try this

Students (or you) maintain all student art work from a given unit or over the course of the year. Student art work can range from thumbnail sketches to well-developed final pieces. A body of work showing the process demonstrates progress over time and provides students with longitudinal reflection. The reflection can take the form of discussions, writing, or video.

I have also incorporated "share chairs" as another option to foster student discussion. Share chairs can look and feel very different depending on the classroom and developmental age of the students, but in short, they are two or three chairs in the classroom where students can go and discuss their work with one or two self-selected peers. At the share chair space, it is helpful to have question stems, a timer, and shared expectations for the space.

Example 2: Options for Sustaining Effort and Persistence

Key questions

Do you share the goal of your lesson in multiple formats? Do you provide options for students to comprehend the desired outcomes?

Try this

After a mini-lesson on reflections found in nature, students hear and read the goal of their independent work time. One student volunteers to share the goal in their own words. Another student is asked to repeat back what the first student said. Then students turn to a partner, share the goal, and explain how they will create a reflection in their artwork. To heighten the salience of the goal, post it in the same location in the classroom for every lesson. At the top margin of all my slides, I post the goal in a green box, so that no matter what students are doing or what we are looking at, the goal is easily accessible.

Example 3: Options for Welcoming Interests and Identities

Key questions

Does your classroom(s) allow students to have flexible seating arrangements? Do you allow options for flexible groupings or for students to work alone? Do students have options to work in more than one medium?

Try this

During a unit on contemporary art, students learn about three different artists and some of their respective works. Students have the autonomy to choose one of three artists' works as inspiration for their piece. Students can use any combination of four different mediums, and they determine the size of the paper or canvas.

> **PAUSE AND THINK**
>
> 1. What are some UDL engagement strategies you are already implementing in your classroom?
> 2. What are the barriers to engagement that your students encounter and which UDL checkpoints could you apply to your lessons to remove or reduce those barriers?

How Do You Respond to Disengagement?

My most challenging art classes are not the ones with the highest number of special education students or the ones full of grudging middle schoolers who do not self-identify as artists but are required to take the class. They are the courses where I have not effectively designed meaningful and authentic curriculum. When students do not connect with the material or know why they should be learning a particular subject, they can present challenges that range from being distracted to demonstrating oppositional behaviors. The barriers, however, are not the students' fault. They are in the design and presentation of my instruction. While I plan with UDL, I sometimes miss the mark and need to be flexible enough to revisit the relevancy of my own instruction.

I never thought I would have a majority of students fail one of my art classes because I try to anticipate potential barriers and develop instruction that reduces those barriers. To my dismay, though, more than 50% of students in one of my seventh-grade classes failed the first quarter many years ago. Throughout the quarter, I spoke with students, their parents, and other teachers about how to best support these students, as their lack of interest in art was palpable.

I tried to improve instruction by applying everything I knew about learning, art, and UDL. Students in the other seventh-grade class were thriving. Both classes had co-created the assessment rubric in which the baseline expectation involved producing art related to the goal and demonstrating appropriate classroom behavior. Eventually I began to provide instruction tailored to this group, yet everything I tried was met with some form of rejection. Like many teachers, I view any student's failure as a reflection of my professional failure and in this case, I was seriously failing to engage numerous students.

Figure 2.5. A student works by lamp light, which creates a calming environment.

After I submitted report cards, my principal wanted to check in and understand how this class earned their grades. I was exhausted, defeated, and in tears as we talked about options for assessment and barriers to their learning. She observed the group and reaffirmed that my instruction was providing multiple options for engagement, representation, and expression, but those options were not targeting the actual barriers. She also noted that one student in the classroom was consuming 85% of my time.

Teaching is emotional work and cannot be done in isolation. In this case, I needed another set of eyes to evaluate instruction, engagement, and their relationship to student behavior, as my own efforts left me emotionally exhausted. Entering the second quarter, and with supportive feedback, I sought to make the content more relevant and engaging. This group needed UDL but not in the same way as other classes aiming toward a similar goal. The "why" for art will likely vary depending on students' developmental needs, school culture, and classroom culture. In the case of my failing seventh graders, they wanted to make something immediately upon entering the classroom. They rebelled against even a two-minute mini-lesson involving demonstrations, videos, visuals, or exemplars. I don't like to have students enter the room and just "create" without knowing the day's goal and learning some component of visual art content to apply to their work. But I had to bend because nothing else was working.

I began the second quarter by placing a minimum of two highly relevant options for art making—based heavily on their personal interests—on each table with visuals, text examples, and directions so that they could immediately begin to make art upon entering the classroom. I did demonstrations at each large table when students began to ask for support, or I did a demonstration at a single table and invited students who were interested in learning a specific skill to come and observe. The demonstrations were either optional or prompted by student questions. We provided the student who had needed 85% of my time an alternative space for art and additional instructional support to meet his needs for making progress. His least restrictive environment, even with UDL, was not an inclusion classroom with only one teacher.

UDL helped me to think about the origin of the discipline challenges and student apathy and design to reduce barriers by applying some of the checkpoints within the guidelines. Without UDL I would not have had a starting place for critically examining my instruction. In the second quarter, all but two students in the class passed art. Those two students were still my "not yets," and I have continued to embed UDL into instruction with the goal of making art a rigorous and accessible class where all students can excel.

It is not a matter of *if*, but *when*, your instruction will be met with disengagement, even if it was planned with UDL. Your teachable moment as a practitioner will come with how you respond to disengagement. Continue to remain flexible and optimistic, re-approach your planning and instruction, and ask for feedback to fuel untapped options, as engagement, relevancy, and authenticity are the cornerstones of meaningful instruction. If students don't care about art or do not understand why it matters, they won't learn or create no matter how many ways you represent content or how many options they have to express their learning.

Designing a Highly Engaging Visual Art Lesson

As a teacher at a pilot school, and now at a standard public school, I have had the gift of relative autonomy over the art content I teach. When I plan a unit or lesson, I begin with a clear UDL goal and determine which National Core Arts Standards or state standards connect to the goal. (If you teach in a private school or in a state that has its own standards, then the NCAS might not be a relevant step in your planning process.)

Once I determine the end-of-unit goal, I think about the barriers students might face and deliberately use the UDL Guidelines to reduce them. Next, I map out individual lessons that build toward attaining the end-of-unit goal. Each lesson often has its own lesson-specific UDL goal. For each lesson, I go through the same process of naming barriers and then developing the methods and assessments. As a final step, I ask myself if the content of the lesson aligns with the unit's goal and if the components of the individual lessons align with their relative goals.

The following lesson focuses on visual art engagement with students in grades 5–8, as middle schoolers can often be challenging to engage. It's based on a contest I was asked to have students enter; arts teachers are often asked to have students do a project, contest, or school-wide work that is out of context for a given unit of study, and the common expectation is that the art teacher can and will stop instruction to meet the needs of a request. Combine a misaligned lesson on a contest with middle schoolers' sometimes apathetic or challenging behaviors, and the art teacher is faced with the ultimate task of engagement. In the case of this lesson, the contest's criteria fit into the current unit on symbolism, and I was able to make a meaningful connection between the objectives of the contest and the goals of the unit.

As you review the lesson, keep in mind that UDL is not a checklist, and a single lesson will not touch upon every checkpoint in the guidelines. Furthermore, this lesson contains aspects related to the representation and expression principles but relates most closely to engagement.

PAUSE AND THINK

1. How might the lesson described below be altered or improved further to reduce barriers and provide more options for engagement?

2. How might this lesson have been presented without UDL, and what impact might that have on students?

 A CLOSER LOOK Visit http://castpublishing.org/skinny-books/art-for-all/resources/ to view the slides and student work associated with this lesson.

ACTIVITY

Lesson title: Diversity Is a Strength: Lesson with an Emphasis on Engagement

Target audience: Students in grades 5–8 (many of the UDL strategies discussed in this lesson could be applied to other grade levels).

Number of classes needed for this lesson: Two or three

Background context: This lesson was a component of a larger unit on the theme of symbolism.

UDL goal: Students will create a work of art that responds to the prompt "Diversity is a strength of our school."

NCAS: The following anchor standards were addressed. The lesson was modified to reflect grade-specific outcomes within each of the anchor standards.

> Anchor Standard 1: Generate and conceptualize artistic ideas and work (Cr1.1, Cr1.2).
>
> Anchor Standard 2: Organize and develop artistic ideas and work (Cr2.3).
>
> Anchor Standard 7: Perceive and analyze artistic work (Re7.2).
>
> Anchor Standard 9: Apply criteria to evaluate artistic work (Re9.1).

Methods:

1. Introduce the concept of diversity with the essential question: What is diversity? Project and read aloud the question. Create a class definition by allowing students to either write their ideas on Post-its and place them on chart paper, share their ideas with a partner, sketch an image, or orally share during a whole-class discussion.

(continued)

2. Examine examples of diversity in context by using visuals and media (use LCD projector). Discuss these essential questions using the same options for participation listed above. Where do you experience diversity in your daily life? Where do you see diversity in the world? What challenges and benefits does society experience when diversity is present? How is diversity represented in our school, and what makes that a strength? Project and read aloud the questions.

3. Connect the lesson to the current unit of study by asking: How could an artist represent diversity with symbols? Project and read aloud the question. Share visuals of symbols that could be interpreted as representing diversity.

4. Share with students the criteria for the contest and the prompt: *Diversity is a strength of our school.* Provide options for representation by having examples of visuals, demonstrations of how to use materials, and the prompt and criteria displayed in text and shared orally.

5. Give students the option of creating a list of action steps and a timeline for this project or using a teacher-made list and timeline.

6. Provide options for creating symbols of diversity: reference images, colors, media, current events.

7. Provide options for creation. This does not need to be literal; students can use words to show diversity.

The engagement guidelines were deliberately implemented by ensuring students had multiple opportunities to connect the project to their personal lives. Students were given options for participating in the lesson and for goal setting and persistence.

(continues)

(continued)

Materials:

Students have the option to use any media that can be applied to a two-dimensional surface: tempera paint, watercolors, watercolor pencils, pen and ink, pencils, pastels, crayons, markers, or collage paper.

The students had the autonomy to choose the materials for their poster so long as the materials were presented on a two-dimensional surface.

Assessment:

Students use a teacher-created rubric to self-evaluate their final poster. They also select a peer to evaluate their work. The teacher will use the same rubric to evaluate the student.

Due to time limitations, the lesson did not provide students with the option of creating their own assessment tool or criteria.

Key Takeaways

- Engaged learners in visual art have a plan for attaining their creative goals and are self-motivated.

- There are countless ways to implement the UDL principle of engagement within the visual arts. Be sure your instruction is targeting a specific barrier and be flexible and willing to re-approach your planning if things aren't working.

- How students interact with their environment impacts their engagement. Creating a universally designed classroom or cart is as critical as planning instruction.

- Culturally Sustaining Pedagogy and Social Emotional Learning play critical roles in UDL implementation.

3

Developing Strategic and Action-Oriented Learners: The "What" of Instruction

Students in my early childhood classes take art just once a week for 45 minutes. A few years ago, I became disheartened that they could only sporadically recall the

Figure 3.1: Second graders examine different representations of drawing birds and insects.

purpose of the previous week's lesson. A goal of the UDL principle of representation is to cultivate learners who are knowledgeable and resourceful, so in starting a new unit on lines I decided to heavily emphasize options for representation to support their transfer of knowledge from week to week.

The primary goals of this unit were to create works of art using various types of line and be able to identify and describe different types of line. We focused on selected works from Lascaux cave art, Wassily Kandinsky, Piet Mondrian, Jackson Pollock, Elaine de Kooning, and the African American abstract expressionist Norman Lewis. We specifically emphasized how lines can make shapes and/or show expression. Key vocabulary words included *horizontal*, *vertical*, *diagonal*, *expression*, and *abstract*.

In each class, we listened to and sang "The Lines Song" from a Scratch Garden YouTube video to learn all about lines. The video had relevant visuals, and during the song, we gradually incorporated hand and arm gestures to show vertical, horizontal, and diagonal lines. We frequently spent a few minutes each period going on "line hunts" looking for examples of these types of lines in the classroom. Students drew representations on Post-its and placed them on the lines they found. More traditionally, we identified these lines in the selected works of art and maintained a classroom anchor chart of the line types.

Knowing the names of the artists was not a primary goal of the lesson, but I provided context for each artist by having students develop a classroom-size history of art timeline, which highlighted the artists and their works with a visual of their place in art history. Students read aloud and viewed images about the artists and their works, and we also spent time exploring and drawing the flags of the countries they were from, emphasizing the use of line in each flag.

The unit had many systematically planned means for engagement and expression. Students began to show comprehension of the concepts from week to week with fewer prompts to help them recall what we had been learning. Students independently sang the line song, made hand gestures, or referred to the visuals of the lines posted in the room or on the anchor chart. They began to lead the lesson by sharing what they already knew about lines and where they had seen different types of lines in their classroom, home, or community. The art classroom was no longer an isolated representation of content. They were becoming learners who resourcefully sought out information and used their knowledge to make connections to pre-existing experiences.

One day several months after our line unit concluded, my principal told me she had just talked with the mother of a boy in my class who was very excited that her son had initiated a conversation about Jackson Pollock. I was thrilled he was retaining what he'd learned and was still talking about it months later. The multiple means of representation I used worked together to support student understanding of the content and he—along with the others—gained meaningful and rigorous exposure to an element of design, developmentally appropriate vocabulary, culturally relevant visuals, and recognized artists. They had become expert learners!

Resourceful and knowledgeable artists know how they learn best and what they need to comprehend content. Students who ask specific questions personify resourceful learning. Students who request materials or a different explanation of a topic are aware of what they know and that they are missing a connection. Students across all age groups who can transfer skills and make generalizations about concepts from one unit of study to the next are knowledgeable artists. If content is taught with minimal forms of representation, students have a much lower chance of accessing background knowledge and gaining the skills to know how they learn and what they need to learn.

In general, you can consider representation to be the "what" of your instruction. How will you represent the content and provide options to support students in their synthesis, transfer, and perception of the material? Multiple means of representation might take the form of

- videos,
- demonstrations,
- draw-alongs,
- stations,
- visuals,
- readings,
- read-alouds, or
- manipulatives.

The list of ways you can present information is seemingly endless. UDL, however, is not a series of strategies. Any of the means of representation mentioned above could be present in a lesson and not incorporated with UDL in mind. You should deliberately and systematically choose to incorporate the means of representation to reduce a foreseen barrier.

A general goal of my instruction is to design lessons and create an environment that fosters student independence, resourcefulness, and creativity. A form of representation I almost always avoid is directly drawing on a student's paper. If I draw something for students, they often perseverate on how I made it look. They also begin to rely on me to do the creating, which leads to classroom management issues, as "helpless" students need unnecessary attention. While drawing for students is a form of representation, it negatively impacts their expression. I systematically plan not to use certain forms of representation, knowing the barriers they present. The UDL principles are teacher led, but in the end, learners develop their own agency and expertise.

PAUSE AND THINK

1. What characterizes a resourceful and knowledgeable artist in your classroom?
2. What means of representation as a teacher do you employ to get students to be resourceful and knowledgeable learners?

Options for Representation

Implementing UDL requires a shift in planning and instruction, and it will reasonably propel you out of your comfort zone. As visual art teachers, however, flexibly thinking about options for representing content will likely be natural for you. The challenge will lie in pushing yourself to go beyond representing your lessons visually.

Imagine that the two-dimensional representation of art is a barrier for your students.

As you consider the means you use to represent the "what" of your instruction, push yourself to provide at least one other option for perceiving and synthesizing information that does not involve two-dimensional visual work.

Start by considering the following general questions when designing the representation of your content as well as brief, lesson-specific examples. (And visit http://castpublishing.org/skinny-books/art-for-all/resources for more practical tips.)

Example 1: Options for Comprehension/Activate Background Knowledge

Key questions

Do you provide options that help students focus on key information? Do you demonstrate the connections and relationships among artists, art history, and the influence of art on society?

Try this

Write the class objectives on the board and use large arrows to point to the specific objective of a given class. When classes rotate, move the arrows to other class's objectives. Within each objective, highlight key vocabulary words and provide a visual when appropriate.

Example 2: Options for Language and Symbols

Key question

Do you present art lessons using multiple visual, physical, and audible formats?

Try this

During a middle school lesson on figure drawing, students are learning about the proportion of the human head to the overall size of the body. The proportion is represented through a visual depicting how many "head lengths" fit into the average body. Students measure their heads and compare the measurement to the length of their bodies, or they use photocopied works of classical art to measure and mark off proportions. They also have the option of using rulers, tape measures, or string to gather information. Finally, they can choose to watch a TED-Ed talk on figure drawing or read about it in an advanced "How to Draw" book.

Example 3: Options for Perception

Key question

Do you provide options for visuals to support information being presented orally?

Try this

During a mini-lesson and read-aloud on Georgia O'Keeffe, the teacher shares the illustrations from a book and has a series of slides showing other examples of O'Keeffe's work that relate to the text. Students examine artificial flowers with cardboard viewfinders and explore how the composition of a flower changes depending on where they position the viewfinder.

SMART TIP Not all students need to learn from the same resources. Empower students to select a resource, work of art, or artifact from a series of options aligned with the same goal.

Implementing UDL has no end, no matter how "good" at it you are. As a heuristic framework, UDL will continue to evolve and improve your teaching practice regardless of how much experience you have. The framework cannot be contained in a box, or on a neat canvas, but at least as artists, many of us are accustomed to dealing with nebulous messiness and approaching problems with creative mindsets. Just keep in mind that while UDL examples can be useful, they are only that—examples. You need to self-check your practice, your biases, your beliefs, and your strategies to explore what works for you but more importantly what works for all your students.

 PAUSE AND THINK

1. What are some UDL representation strategies that you are already implementing in your classroom?

2. What are the barriers to representation that your students encounter, and which checkpoints could you apply to your lessons to reduce or remove those barriers?

Experimenting With 3D Construction

Upon transitioning to a new school, I embarked on a journey to revamp my instructional approach. This could seem overwhelming, but I took my own advice and made adjustments at a sustainable pace, aiming to reduce and remove the most significant barriers first. Notably, my middle school students grappled with disengagement and self-doubt regarding their artistic abilities. Given our limited budget, I proposed a curriculum centered on 3D construction using recycled materials like cardboard and hot glue. The ensuing 10-week unit on 3D art proved transformative, igniting unprecedented student engagement.

Initially, I introduced students to various cardboard connection techniques by creating abstract pieces inspired by abstract concepts. While students grasped the technical aspects well, their creations leaned towards literal interpretations like boats and houses. Recognizing the need for more exposure to abstract art and catering to their interests, I refined the curriculum the following year. Students were presented with six options for their projects, each requiring intricate cardboard constructions. Students needed more options for representation of what abstract 3D art could look like, as well as other options for understanding the techniques. I created 3D anchor charts, designed checklists with visuals, compiled key vocabulary lists, and enhanced the existing forms of representation with culturally relevant artists. These adjustments not only honored their preferences but also elevated the level of challenge, resulting in all students meeting the set goals with remarkable creations.

Building on this success, we delved into 3D abstract art, leveraging students' newfound skills and enthusiasm.

Once we incorporated additional examples and interactive activities focused on interpreting abstract art, students embraced the abstract form more readily, leading to a shift towards less literal artistic expressions.

This iterative process of adapting instruction based on student feedback and preferences exemplifies the essence of Universal Design for Learning, fostering inclusivity and maximizing student potential.

An Art Lesson With Multiple Means of Representation

I have found that the most successful art "instruction" and art classes often occur when I have a clear goal with flexible means, and I focus my planning on providing multiple access points to a general goal, theme, artist, historical period, or guiding question. The instruction becomes the multiple means of representation that allows students to experience art in an environment and within a curriculum with fewer barriers. It is in this context that more of my students flourish. The following lesson emphasizes multiple means of representation. While it is intended for a middle school or secondary audience, the concepts and forms of representation could be applied to much younger audiences.

 A CLOSER LOOK Go online to view the slides and student work associated with this lesson.

PAUSE AND THINK

1. Read the lesson that follows and ask yourself how it might be altered or further improved to reduce barriers and provide more options for representation.

2. How might this lesson have been presented without UDL and what impact might that have on students?

ACTIVITY

Lesson title: Masks in Many Contexts: Lesson with an Emphasis on Representation

Target audience: Students in grades 6-12 (many of the UDL strategies discussed in this lesson could be applied to other grade levels).

Number of classes needed for this lesson: Three or four

Background context: This lesson was a component of a larger unit on the culture and contexts of masks.

UDL goal: Students will create a skull mask in the context of Dia de Los Muertos (Day of the Dead). Their work should represent one or more of their positive characteristics or qualities that they might mask or subdue.

NCAS: The following anchor standards were addressed. The lesson was modified to reflect grade-specific outcomes within each of the anchor standards.

Anchor Standard 1: Generate and conceptualize artistic ideas and work (Cr1.1, Cr1.2).
Anchor Standard 2: Organize and develop artistic ideas and work (Cr2.1).

(continues)

(continued)

Anchor Standard 7: Perceive and analyze artistic work (Re7.1, Re7.2).

Anchor Standard 11: Relate artistic ideas and works with societal, historical, and cultural context to deepen understanding (Cn11.1).

Methods:

1. Refer to the anchor chart describing content students already learned during the mask unit (this is similar to a KWL chart, which would be an effective alternative). Introduce the concept of Dia de Los Muertos by showing an image and asking the class if anyone has any experience or knowledge of this celebration and would like to share. The teacher or a student records any comments shared on the anchor chart. Translate Dia de los Muertos to English if a student has not already done so.

2. Project a map of North America and Central America. Discuss and identify where Dia de Los Muertos began. Project images of the masks and painted faces. Have students either record an emotional reaction to the images on a Post-it or determine a movement or sound that represents their reaction. Students share their responses in small groups. Show students a short YouTube clip on Dia de los Muertos. Ask students to consider how their initial reaction to the masks might differ from someone celebrating Dia de los Muertos. Student volunteers can share their initial reaction with how people who celebrate Dia de los Muertos might respond to the masks. Compare and contrast the reactions.

(continued)

3. Ask students to now consider their own positive skills or characteristics that they might "mask" but should celebrate. If relevant, discuss how peer pressure can influence social behaviors and decisions, and provide visuals, relevant readings, and/or video clips to support this conversation if needed. Have students sketch, write, and/or think of a symbolic movement, pose, or gesture to represent one or more of their positive characteristics. Have students share in small groups, and have several students share whole class.

4. Ask students to determine how they might represent these characteristics on a mask in the genre of Dia de los Muertos. Share the goal with the class by reading it aloud and projecting it.

5. Show students the various representations for planning their mask.

6. Students have the remainder of class and the next class to plan their masks, brainstorm and create images, draw patterns, or use text to represent the characteristics of themselves that they might mask.

7. During the next two or three lessons on the masks of Dia de los Muertos, begin class with a brief discussion, video, images, Q and A, or jigsaw to further support students in gaining a deeper understanding of the meaning and context of the masks and celebration.

8. When students have completed the planning process, they can develop and transfer their ideas to one of several mask molds or create their own.

(continues)

(continued)

9. Students have the option of sharing their mask during small-group or whole-class critiques. The planning pieces and the final piece should become a part of their portfolios.

The representation guidelines were deliberately implemented by ensuring students had multiple opportunities to activate prior knowledge, transfer knowledge from one concept to another, clarify vocabulary and represent content using multiple media, and offer alternatives to visual and auditory information.

Materials:

Students have the autonomy to use any media that can be applied to the surface of the mask: collage images and paper, found objects, Mod Podge, tempera paint, watercolors, watercolor pencils, pen and ink, pencils, pastels, crayons, and markers.

Assessment:

Students use a generalizable rubric they created at the beginning of the year to evaluate their work. During the end-of-unit critique, peers will review three pieces from their portfolio using the rubric. The teacher will provide students with qualitative and formative feedback during work sessions in the form of notes and discussions.

Key Takeaways

- You will know your students are learners with agency within the principle of representation when they know *what* they need to learn and create.

- Visual art naturally lends itself to multiple forms of representation; however, the principle of representation goes far beyond the superficial teaching strategies of showing students visuals.

4

Helping Artists Show What They Know: The "How" of Instruction

During a first-grade art class, a student with autism incoherently began to obsess over a social interaction. I attempted a half dozen interventions, but he was

Figure 4.1: First graders express themselves using self-made puppets and sets.

not responsive. In a final bid to support this student, I reached for a stuffed gorilla, mistakenly named Mr. Monkey by students. I held him up and became an amateur ventriloquist; the gorilla repeated the questions I was asking, but this time the student's entire physical and emotional presence de-escalated. The first grader and Mr. Monkey went on to have the most sophisticated and insightful conversation I had witnessed from him all year.

Other students in the class approached Mr. Monkey and began to ask questions and make detailed observations. I was thrilled with the spontaneously complex discussions Mr. Monkey and the students were having, as increasing the level of student-to-student discourse has been a school-wide goal and is an area of personal and professional interest for me. From that interaction, I planned puppet-making and puppetry as the next unit for the first and second grade as I wanted to give all students the opportunity to have uninhibited conversations with their own puppet.

As I mentioned earlier, a majority of my students at Gardner Pilot Academy are English language learners, and as a full-inclusion Boston public school, approximately 25% of our student body have an identified disability, with 10% having disabilities that would typically keep them from the mainstream classroom. Beyond these characteristics, there are a variety of curricular barriers that sometimes inhibit student talk. Students in my first- and second-grade art classes had been typically engaging in single-word or simple-sentence responses to questions. Within a conversation, most students either lacked the skills to participate in a complex discussion or were conversationally timid. The puppetry unit gave many of them the means for communicating with confidence as well as a format to practice storytelling.

The unit began with a class on planning their puppets. Students then had several classes to self-select materials to design a puppet. We reviewed story elements using multiple means of representation and students created a set, plot, and dialogue for their story. Presenting their stories was optional, but 100% of students were eager to share their art and speak in front of the class.

Puppets were a catalyst for learning about storytelling and the art of puppet making. More importantly, my students were taking conversational risks, growing their vocabularies, and authentically practicing sustained

Figure 4.2: A student's plan for her puppet

discourse. We used the puppets as an option for a means of communication for the remainder of the year, as the positive influence of puppetry extended far beyond the end of the unit.

The principles of action and expression aim to help learners become strategic and goal directed. They know how they can most effectively show what they learned. Applying UDL to my teaching helped me to notice barriers and determine flexible means for overcoming those barriers. In this case, the barrier was not autism or second language learning; it was that the options for expression were limited. Providing students with puppets increased the ways they could communicate, and for many students, speaking through a paper bag or paper plate puppet unlocked their voice, not only increasing student-to-student discourse but supporting their storytelling skills while planning and creating characters for their puppets. Increasing options for expression gave them more opportunities to become strategic learners and increased the likelihood they would gain confidence in their skills and set self-directed goals.

PAUSE AND THINK

What characterizes a strategic and goal-directed artist in your classroom?

Options for Expression

The boundary between right and wrong in the arts may be blurred in comparison to more definitive content areas, but making visual art more accessible to all students is

HELPING ARTISTS SHOW WHAT THEY KNOW 67

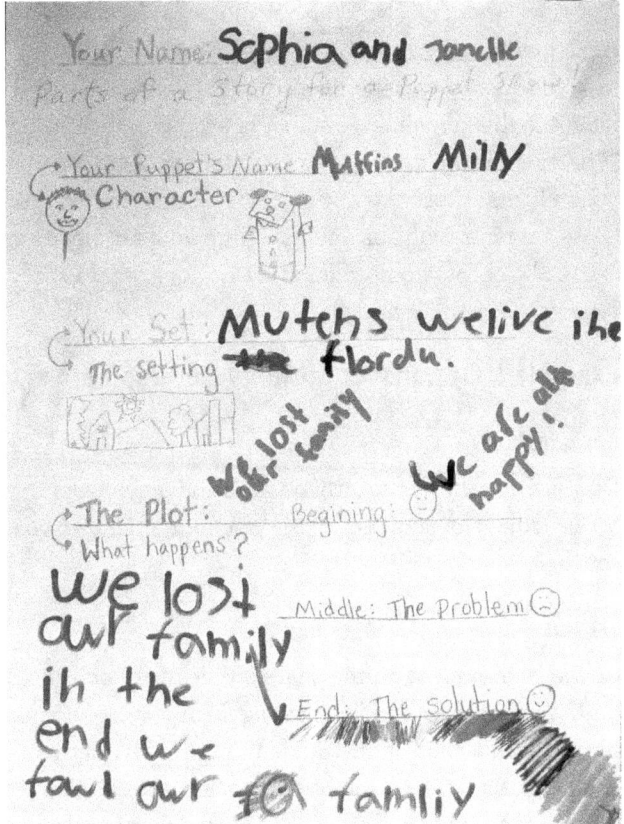

Figure 4.3: A planning template students used for outlining their stories

just as vital. UDL is not a deficit model, it helps reframe your thinking about students' skills and potential. Students are not lacking ability; the curriculum is disabled. Reducing or removing barriers does not make the content any less rigorous, it merely allows students to gain access to information while helping students learn *how* they learn, not just what to learn.

Below are some general questions to support your implementation of the principle of expression as well as some lesson-specific ideas. UDL examples can help illustrate the guidelines, but examples can be confining. Whatever examples of UDL you find meaningful, remind yourself that those are options for all students, not just those students who absolutely require another means to learn. The cornerstone belief of UDL is that what is good for some is good for all.

Example 1: Options for Strategy Development

Key question

Do you model how to set artistic goals and provide options for structures for students to use to support their own goal setting?

Try this

At the beginning of a unit, share a timeline of objectives for the unit and a calendar showing the number of classes before the final piece is due. Students need to set three measurable goals between the beginning and end of the unit. They have the option of annotating the timeline or calendar or completing a graphic organizer using images or text.

Example 2: Options for Expression and Communication

Key question

If a lesson requires specific use of one type of media, do you allow students to have other media-related options such as the surface or type of paper they work on, the scale of their work, or mark-making tools?

Try this

In a lesson on watercolor painting techniques, students are expected to use a paint brush and watercolor; they can choose, however, the size of the brush, use a pencil grip on the brush handle, and/or can choose the size of the watercolor paper. In addition, students have the option of using a picture and text-based graphic organizer to support their work. Students also engage in both turn-and-talks and a whole-class discussion on the techniques, supported by an anchor chart that they can optionally reference during independent work time.

Example 3: Options for Interaction

Key questions

Do students have options to vary the timing, rate, and speed of the creative process? Do students have options for participating in discussions?

Try this

Students have the option to respond to AP art questions using Plickers or Post-its. Students can express follow-up questions orally, post them to a Padlet, or post them to a class anchor chart. There are planned segments in each lesson for students to discuss questions and answers in small groups, with the teacher, or via a form of technology.

> **PAUSE AND THINK**
>
> 1. How can you provide learners with options for expression that are aligned with the goal, rigorous, and also an alternative to the typical means you present during your instruction?
>
> 2. How can you set up a curriculum and environment to help students learn how they learn?

"Art Is When _____?"

Art teachers know first-hand how challenging it can be to inspire and instruct a variable group of students. Anyone who has tried to teach a group of students why the arts matter and how to create a work of art knows that some of the students readily access the content and some encounter numerous barriers to experiencing success.

By designing instruction with the UDL Guidelines, you can systematically plan for these barriers. When faced with the predictable statements of "I'm not an artist" or "I can't do this," consider other options for expression. Before my first year as a visual art teacher, I knew these self-identifying statements would resonate with some of my students. When the school year began, I asked every class "What is art?" Each class contributed to a school-wide graphic organizer displaying their varying responses to this question. Over the course of the year, we continued to add to the visual. I frequently found myself asking the students who didn't identify as artists to reference it. Asking students to consider this question supported those with limited views of visual art.

In the following year, I asked all students to consider the question "Art is when_____?" With a philosophical twist on the previous year's question, students were pushed to think about the actions associated with visual art. The question was a play on philosopher Nelson Goodman's "When is art?" (1976). I inverted the question because a literal interpretation of the question was an inherent barrier. I felt students would naturally answer the question with the day and time of their art class, as opposed to considering other interpretations.

Some of my other methods for providing students with multiple options for expression included the general emphasis on process over product. Any piece that students created in class became part of their portfolios. Students reviewed their portfolios at the conclusion of the unit and could select any work to further develop or present as a final piece. All students, even preschoolers, had portfolio reviews. Maintaining 400 portfolios required some universally designed organizational systems. I found the most efficient and reliable method for cataloging their artwork was to use a binder clip for each class's work and a Post-it note labeling their cohort and grade. Twice a year, students reviewed their portfolios and took their work home after the portfolio review.

During the year, each grade level presented their work in the school "gallery" space, which was the hallway outside of the art room with an alliterative sign naming it after our school mascot: "The Gardner Griffin Gallery." Students were curators of this space. They "framed" their pieces on black cardboard and arranged the installations. Being a curator was sometimes a role that the typically disengaged students enjoyed because they had the option to participate in art without actually making something. The gallery space became a meaningful source of expression.

In addition to presenting artwork in the gallery, 100% of students needed to select a piece from their portfolio for a school-wide art show. Having a breadth of work to choose from engaged all but four students in the school. The four students who did not want to participate had several 1:1 meetings with me to discuss why they did not want to present artwork in the show. Two of the students said they did not want their names on the piece. This was an easy barrier to overcome, as it was not relevant to presenting in the show. These students chose to be anonymous. The other two students felt that none of their art was "good enough" and one of the two students dramatically ripped up her portfolio, sabotaging the expectation that everyone had work to present. We revisited the "What is art?"

Figure 4.4. A fifth-grade class engages with the school-wide art show by taking notes, making sketches, participating in discussions, asking questions, and leaving feedback for the artists.

board and I asked both to consider selecting a piece to improve or consider beginning a new piece. I encouraged them to look for inspiration from their peers' artwork and provided them with more explicit art instruction and other sources for motivation. With additional options for expression, both students created a new piece for the show. The barriers were reduced, and we achieved 100% participation in the show.

 SMART TIP To keep your instruction rigorous, use options to support access to a means-specific goal. If the goal is to present your work or compose a statement, work to provide options to all students that will allow them to excel while engaging in a productive struggle.

All students were expected to create an artist's statement for their piece in the show. Predictable barriers were that some students were non-writers, and many students did not have context for what artist statements should include. To proactively plan for these barriers, I created seven different statement templates to support their writing. These templates included various combinations of word boxes, sentence starters, and assorted fonts and line sizes. Mini-lessons included multiple means for representing what statements can be. Students who were not yet writers orally shared their statements but still had the option of guiding their ideas with sentence starters. Some students chose to record their statements using Photobooth, an app that easily records videos. Other students presented them using puppets and then either used a scribe or wrote their ideas on a template.

With so many choices, I expected many students to choose the "easier" options. While this occurred with several grudging middle schoolers, many students selected a "just right" template. Some of the students who appeared to be taking a less rigorous option asked me if they could transfer their statements from the "easier" template to the template that only had blank lines. When I asked why, they said they wanted to start with something they thought they could do and then try the harder one. If I had pre-determined who would receive which template, I would have deprived them of the opportunity to learn how they learn and what they need to learn. I engaged students who stuck with unnecessarily simplistic templates in a discussion about making more appropriate choices in the future. Becoming a strategic, action-oriented learner takes time and multiple exposures to many means of expression. It is not always reasonable to assume all students will always choose the best option for themselves, but without providing them options, they will never have that chance.

Soon after publishing the first edition, I re-examined my students' artist statements. While I had 100% of students writing about their art, their statements represented simplistic writing and often did not demonstrate their creative journey or the deeper meaning behind their art. As with all things UDL, I knew the barrier to improving the quality of their writing was within the "what" and "how" I was teaching, not a deficit on their part.

Upon reflection, I realized that some of the options I had provided them with directed their writing with a heavy hand and resulted in trite, algorithmic descriptions of their art. Having 100% participation in writing a statement was no longer satisfactory.

I realized that I had left out one of the cornerstones of options for representation when it comes to writing. I had not provided them with options for exemplars. To remedy this, I curated six different works of art, both contemporary and historical, and found the corresponding artists' impression or actual statement. The next time I had students write artist statements, I had the class look at the six pieces of art and we took a vote on which one they wanted to learn more about. Once the vote was determined, I projected the corresponding statement and passed out a packet with all six statements. As a class we did a close reading of the statement; students chose to follow along on the screen or in paper form. A close reading is a structured approach to reading that helps students extract meaning from complex texts by repeatedly reading an excerpt and can involve annotating the text and answering text-based questions. Close reading moves beyond comprehension into inferential understanding of the text, allowing students to engage with the nuances and deeper meaning of the text.

After studying the exemplar artist statement, students had the option of reading or listening to any of the other five statements, and they could engage in this alone or with one or two peers. Students then did a jigsaw, where they shared what they learned with students who had read about a different work of art. At the conclusion, as a class, we compiled a list of characteristics of strong statements. Students then used this list to write their artist statement. More open-ended sentence stems and graphic organizers were also provided as options to support their expression.

The results were artist statements that were profound and creative, and contributed to the viewer fully experiencing and understanding each work of art. Students were also more eager to write their statements, as many of them had felt stifled by the previous instruction. This is just one example of how UDL is truly an iterative process in which we design to reduce and remove barriers, which in turn sometimes reveals other barriers in our design.

 A CLOSER LOOK   Visit http://castpublishing.org/skinny-books/art-for-all/resources/ to view artist statement templates.

"This Class Sucks": Welcoming All Feedback

It is a very rare day when all students choose the same means for expressing their creativity. Similarly, students express their emotions and feedback in multiple ways. Oral check-ins and whole-class discussions are typical forms of expression. I also provide a comment box in my classroom. Students use the comment box to share feedback on lessons, make requests for art projects, and vent about life in general. The box is anonymous, which means it is inevitable that at some point in the year a student will write "This class sucks" or some other version of disdain for art or myself. It is also almost just as certain that younger students will express their undying love for art or me in somewhat legible handwriting.

Having the outlet of a comment box can help students self-regulate in the classroom. The comments often describe barriers students face and areas for professional growth. When I see a class more than once a week, I often read all the comments aloud (pending appropriate language). I have a discussion with students focused on their ideas and how I will tailor instruction to their feedback.

As an exit ticket, I occasionally ask students to write down on a Post-it something that is going well in art and something that could be going better. I sort them into categories, photograph them, and show them to the class. Not all students choose to participate, and as with the comment box, some middle schoolers love to write "nothing" as a response to both questions.

Yet there are valuable insights in their feedback. They name barriers such as the "messiness" of art or the noise in the classroom, barriers that I am sometimes oblivious to. I do my best not to take these comments personally, but rather reflect on them professionally. When negative feedback becomes a pattern, those comments can help drive professional growth. Our students are the people we serve. If what I am doing isn't working, I need to fix it or make it more accessible. Giving them options for expressing their feedback allows them multiple means for sharing those thoughts, while improving my teaching practice.

An Art Lesson With Multiple Means of Action and Expression

If you begin your planning with a clear goal and identify potential barriers, you will be able to design lessons that allow students multiple options for attaining the goal. Before planning a unit on patterns for early childhood art classes, I determined that a major barrier would be creating developmentally complex patterns, transferring knowledge of patterns from one medium to another, and understanding the concept of repetition. I planned the unit with an emphasis on multiple means of expression so that students would have numerous methods for showing what they knew about patterns.

> **A CLOSER LOOK** Visit http://castpublishing.org/skinny-books/art-for-all/resources/ to view the slides and student work associated with this lesson.

ACTIVITY

Lesson title: Creating Patterns: Lesson with an Emphasis on Expression

Target audience: Students in preschool to second grade (many of the UDL strategies discussed in this lesson could be applied to other grade levels).

Number of lessons: Two or three

Background context: This lesson occurred during the second half of a unit on patterns. Many of the options for expression had been introduced and practiced during individual lessons that occurred in the first half of the unit.

UDL goal: Students will create patterns using shapes, colors, letters, and/or numbers.

(continued)

NCAS: The following anchor standards were addressed. The lesson was modified to reflect grade-specific outcomes within each of the anchor standards.

Anchor Standard 1: Generate and conceptualize artistic ideas and work (Cr1.2).

Anchor Standard 2: Organize and develop artistic ideas and work (Cr2.1).

Anchor Standard 3: Refine and complete artistic work (Cr3.1).

Anchor Standard 4: Select, analyze, and interpret artistic works for presentation (Pr4.1).

Methods:

1. Students sit on the rug. Each student receives one of three types of pattern blocks. One student is asked to put their block in the middle of the circle. Then a second student is chosen to place their pattern block down on the rug next to the other block. The teacher asks, If the pattern were to repeat, what would go next? Students with those blocks contribute to the pattern. Variations of patterns are created with several rounds of this activity.

2. The teacher asks students to turn and talk and describe what the word *repeat* means. One to two students share an example and identify repetition in a pattern. The teacher asks students if they see any patterns in the classroom or on their clothes.

(continues)

(continued)

3. Students are told they are going to watch a YouTube video of monks making a mandala. A mandala is a Buddhist or Hindu symbol often composed of circles and intricate patterns. Students practice saying the word *monks* and *mandala*. They watch the video and look for patterns. The video is played once without stopping. At the conclusion, the teacher asks students where they saw a pattern. The video is played again and paused on an image of the mandala. Students describe patterns they see. The class discusses the cultural context of the mandala, and students hypothesize what material is being used to make the mandala.

4. Students are told that they are going to be making mandalas, but there are a lot of ways to make them. The teacher shares visuals, shows short demos of each method, and posts examples of each method on the board:

   - Make a mandala with a partner or by yourself using pattern blocks or plastic shapes. (Discuss how these pieces are ephemeral.)
   - Create your own mandala pattern using any of the materials.
   - Use a mandala template to show patterns with color.
   - Use the blocks to make a mandala and then trace it onto paper.
   - Use pre-cut paper shapes or craft supplies to make a mandala.
   - Contribute to the whole-class mandala by meeting with the teacher to continue a pattern started by your classmate.

(continued)

5. Students are also reminded that if they want to continue to work on a work of art on patterns from a previous week, they can. Those options include patterns with numbers, letters, and palindromes.

6. Students work on one or more of the options for expression. They can transition to another option at their own pace.

7. Students clean up materials and return to the rug. Students have the option to share their work with a peer. The prompts for the share are reviewed using visuals, hand gestures, and oral language. Students are asked to tell their partner one part of their work that they think is strong. Students ask each other how their art makes them feel and then ask each other a question about their work.

Materials:

Students have options to use crayons, oil pastels, colored pencils, pattern blocks, magnet tiles, transparent plastic shapes, LEGO bricks, craft manipulatives, predrawn mandala templates, and pattern prediction sheets.

Assessment:

Students join the teacher in small groups at a station where there are a series of patterns started. Students are asked to choose one of the patterns and continue it. Students are asked to describe how they know what comes next and to explain what the word *repeat* means.

(continues)

(continued)

> Student work is examined to identify each student's proficiencies with pattern representations with regards to accuracy and complexity.
>
> Students share one of their pieces at the end of class and/or at the end of the unit and explain their pattern while also asking their peers at least one question about their art (or making at least one comment depending on the developmental stage of the student).

A Note About AI and Art Instruction

Since the first edition was published, artificial intelligence, in particular generative AI, has provided educators with numerous opportunities for enhancing instruction both in its breadth and efficiency. Art educators can use AI tools like ChatGPT, Bard, or any paid subscription service in numerous ways. Asking AI for suggestions for artists and artworks that align with a goal and represent my student body is one of its most helpful features for me. Instead of sometimes spending hours searching Google, I find that generative AI does most of the work, and after revising my initial prompt, I typically get better information than if I had scoured websites and blogs. Teachers can also use it to generate lesson plans, test questions, and even emails to parents. Depending on your school's policy for technology use, students can use AI to support their learning by asking specific questions related to a creative challenge (Roose, 2023).

I've also, on occasion, found AI to be helpful when trying to determine teacher moves that would support UDL. I ask AI for options to reduce or remove a given learning barrier in relation to a goal. While the results never fully answer my question and sometimes involve methods and strategies I've already tried, I often get ideas for improving instruction. This does not mean you can type in "Create a UDL visual art lesson for sixth graders on one-point perspective" and expect your lesson to be thoughtfully designed with UDL, as AI does not know the specific variability of your students.

LUDIA is an AI-powered chatbot designed to support educators in implementing UDL. It offers educators efficient ways to integrate UDL principles into their teaching and provides context-specific and culturally sustainable suggestions for instructional design based on the UDL Guidelines.

When using LUDIA, educators can do the following:

1. Describe the diversity of their learners and potential barriers to learning.

2. Present their instructional goals and challenges.

3. Receive UDL-aligned suggestions and strategies.

LUDIA analyzes this input and generates recommendations drawn from a vast knowledge base of UDL research and best practices. This allows educators to quickly access targeted, UDL-aligned strategies to improve learning outcomes for all students.

While LUDIA is a powerful tool for UDL implementation, it's important to note that it complements rather than replaces the educator's expertise and experience. The nuanced application of UDL principles still requires human insight, creativity, and understanding of individual learner needs that AI cannot fully replicate. LUDIA serves as a valuable resource and scaffold, empowering educators to enhance their UDL practice while maintaining their essential role in the learning process.

To further develop your use of AI, I suggest checking out *A Teachers Prompt Guide to ChatGPT* (CESE, 2023). It offers more ideas for how educators can use AI both with planning and for students to use in the classroom. The ideas discussed in this teacher-friendly resource are transferable to any Generative AI platform.

 Key Takeaways

- When students have goal-oriented options for action and expression, they are able to engage in rigorous instruction while having the flexibility to fully express their creativity.

- There's no place for cookie-cutter art lessons when instruction incorporates multiple means for action and expression.

- Options for action and expression in visual art extend far beyond the actual creation of a work of art. Students are empowered to self-assess, self-reflect, and create personalized learning goals.

- Generative AI can be an effective tool for supporting UDL implementation.

5

The Burnt Banana (and Other Professional Learning Moments)

Figure 5.1: A burnt banana, fried after multiple experimental rounds of reheating in my classroom's microwave (photo credit: Ms. Kat A-P)

It was May of my last year teaching math before moving to my newly created visual art teaching position. My UDL practice was in full force; part of my weekly instruction involved offering students seven math options for demonstrating comprehension of that week's primary goal. Students had complete autonomy over who they worked with and where they sat. They also had autonomy over which options they started with and how long they worked at each choice. With frequent check-ins and feedback, qualitative and quantitative data showed that students were taking more responsibility for their learning and gaining grade-level math skills.

One morning I smelled something odd while working with a group of students. "Do you smell anything?" I asked the sixth graders. They flashed subtle, mischievous smirks. "No." But only moments later, several students giddily shrieked: "Ms. Byron, look!"

> **A CLOSER LOOK** For a bonus chapter, visit http://castpublishing.org/skinny-books/art-for-all/resources/ and see "Multiple Perspectives on One-Point Perspective"—a detailed example of using UDL in lesson planning.

The students had pulled back the curtain that concealed our classroom microwave. Puffs of smoke escaped the seams of the microwave's plastic door. I opened it up to find part of my lunch incinerated into a pile of black mush.

"Everyone back to your seats. Who did this?" I asked. Anxious that the fire alarm might be set off, I instructed two students to open the windows.

As I did so, my colleague and evaluator came into the room, incredulous. "What is going on?"

"Well, I think there was a small fire," I reported.

She glanced at the microwave and instantly laughed, which also sparked an uncontrollable coughing fit as there was still smoke in the air. We debriefed in the open doorway, where she good-naturedly helped me appreciate the absurdity.

Up to this moment, everything in my classroom had been consistently improving, and most students were engaged and learning. The autonomy and choices contributed to stronger student learning outcomes. But they also gave students the idea that they could experiment with the temperature at which bananas burn. The latter was not in my lesson plan. Was this a failure in my classroom management? Was it simply middle schoolers being noncompliant, curious, or devious? Or was this a result of implementing UDL beyond my present abilities? I might have avoided the burnt banana by minimizing choice, but I'm glad I did not, partly because the fire alarm did not go off and partly because you can't make progress without some failure.

I like to think the burnt banana represents pushing the bounds of UDL to the edge of my professional practice while demonstrating the innate curiosity of the preteen. It also demonstrates how we cannot possibly plan for everything. We will all have our own "burnt bananas" when implementing UDL. Let's just hope the burning is more from igniting the fire of learning and less from a literal fire.

Here are some other lessons I've learned.

The Elephant in the Room

When implementing UDL, we talk about barriers to learning being within our curriculum and physical classroom environment, but what I've learned since publishing the first edition of this book is that the biggest barrier to learning is often us, the educators. Don't take this personally, but you (and me!) can inadvertently derail a lesson, create resistance to learning, or sidetrack your students. The elephant in the room often takes the form of our implicit bias as well as our personal identities and how they influence instruction and create walls to fully incorporating Culturally Sustaining Pedagogy and UDL.

Implicit bias is the attitude or stereotypes that unconsciously affect our understanding, actions, and decisions. This last part, the unconscious part, is the trickiest, as it's hard to know what you inherently don't see or notice. And the reality is that no matter how you identify, everyone has implicit bias (Project Implicit, 2024; Starck et al., 2020). Furthermore, there is extensive research demonstrating that students who look like their teachers do better in school (Boisrond, 2017; Egalite & Kisida, 2017; Gershenson et al., 2017; Lindsay & Hart, 2017; Vinopal & Holt, 2019).

When I first read these studies, I became defensive, as almost none of my students are white. I interpreted the studies as saying I must be a bad teacher because of my race. Looking back, what a predictable and painful reaction: the white teacher is a victim of her race. I had taken the data personally and withdrew, but in reflection realized, that, because I have such vastly different experiences as a white middle-class, heterosexual, cisgender female, I have that much more of a responsibility to unearth my biases, so I began genuinely working on exposing my biases.

So how do I know when my implicit biases impact student learning? After really honing my CSP instruction, I have students who will challenge my teaching moves and/or content because they feel comfortable questioning how and why things happen in the classroom. But before I could get there, I relied on intense reflective practices. Even after publishing a book on UDL instruction, I still had (and have) many occasions where I had planned with UDL and had created what I thought was a fantastic set of lessons, only to have them not go off with the fireworks I had anticipated. And when this happens, I've come to realize that I am more often the barrier that hadn't been addressed. This is my canary in the classroom: if you've genuinely designed with UDL, and the outcome is underwhelming at best, then consider yourself and your implicit biases the barriers.

Here's an example of the subtleties of implicit bias. After the pandemic, I taught eighth grade for the first period of the day and my school's start time is 7:15 AM. Getting to school on time for a 13-year-old who is likely using public transit is a huge challenge, combined with the fact that biologically they aren't meant to wake up this early (American Psychological Association, 2023; Heissel & Norris, 2019). I wanted to ensure my eighth graders who arrived on time (at first, this was about 30% of the class) knew how impressed I was with them. At the onset of class, I would proudly say, "You are all going to get and keep a job, and you are going to be respected employees because you are already showing the dedication and responsibility needed in a professional setting."

Now, I had no bad intention in what I said, but on reflection, I realized that my implicit bias had impacted my word choice. Why wasn't I saying, "You are going to be CEOs, leaders of companies, and presidents of organizations by showing up on time, ready to learn at such an early hour." For some subtle, unconscious reason, my language reverted to "employee" and not "CEO." Once I realized this, I apologized to the class and explained why I was sorry. We then talked about what a CEO is and how their timeliness already makes them great leaders.

The second half of this story involves the other 70% of the students who were arriving anywhere from 5 to 30 minutes late (or sometimes not at all!). My upbringing and identity impacted my assumptions about these students. I figured they should be able to get to school on time, no excuses. While being on time should be the expectation, when students aren't on time, finding out the barriers to meeting the goal is critical.

Instead of simply demanding that my latecomers get to school earlier, I started by warmly welcoming them when they did arrive, noting that I was glad they were here and immediately pointing them in the direction of the goal for the project and reviewing the content they missed (or having another student share it). I assumed that if students got engaged and knew what they were missing and that they were not being "hated on" the moment they walked in, they would start to arrive on time. Many latecomers quickly began to say, "What? I only have 10 minutes to work!?" and my response would be to prioritize waking up earlier.

For some students, just the realization that they wanted more time to work on an engaging project got them in the door earlier. For other students, it wasn't enough. I asked students about their morning and evening routines, at-home responsibilities, and transportation. I asked them what they thought was making their arrival difficult. With each individual situation (now about 30% of the class), we problem-solved, and for some students, we set a more attainable goal of arriving only 15 minutes late at first. I never had 100% of my eighth graders arrive on time, but got closer to 80%, with the other 20% trickling in and getting right to work. The atmosphere in the class, however, was never one of distrust that they weren't trying, it was one of welcoming, understanding, and problem-solving.

Through my bias and assumptions, I've created countless barriers for my students, and the most challenging thing is that I am often not aware of them. So how can we as educators start to reduce or remove this barrier? First, ask your students for feedback, and look for responses that might reveal that they feel disconnected from the content or goals or even from you. Ask a peer to observe you and openly discuss how you want to unpack your biases with your evaluator. Debrief tricky lessons with a colleague and explicitly look for areas where bias might have interfered.

We can produce very different reactions from our students just by varying the tone of our voice and being deliberate with our word choice (Paulmann & Weinstein, 2022). Consider how your biases impact your tone and word choice and how those can be the barrier to student learning. Keep in mind that our biases extend far beyond the physical attributes of race or perceived gender identity. Socio-economic status is a better predictor of need or privilege than the color of our skin (Hughes, 2024).

In the words of Jay Smooth, exposing and diminishing the negative impact of implicit bias and prejudice is comparable to removing the plaque on our teeth: we must work at cleaning it off every day. "And just as good oral hygiene does not guarantee we will never have bad breath or have food stuck in our teeth, regular questioning, learning, and engaging across differences can only decrease how much our bias and prejudice show up in our daily thoughts, words, and actions. We accept this reality and keep practicing" (Lee, 2015; Smooth, 2011).

"I Want to Do What I Was Doing"

A second-grade student crawled and jumped around the art room during a mini-lesson when he was expected to be with his class sitting on the rug, a stool, or standing. I set a timer, gave him a break, and offered alternative seating and fidget toys. He ignored my forms of communication. During group and independent work, he continued to meander around the classroom making mechanical gestures and vocalizations.

I asked him why he wasn't participating.

"Because I don't want to."

"What do you want to do?" I asked, hoping he would reveal some interests that I could use to engage him.

"I want to do what I was doing."

"Well, what were you doing?" I asked.

"I was a fighting robot," he said.

I attempted to have him engage with the lesson by taking on a tableau of a more pacifist version of his robot character, but he refused. I asked if he would critique a peer's work, paint with a peer or me, use different mediums, or act out being a robot in a landscape. None of this was appealing, and he stuck to his own goal.

While he was not disrupting the learning environment, my implementation of UDL failed with this student; he was not engaged in any activity related to the goal. My professional understanding and application of multiple means of engagement, representation, and expression were insufficient.

When your practice of UDL does not seem to work, reevaluate the lesson, check in with the students, and create plans that continue to reduce barriers. When that does not work the first time, be ready to revisit the drawing board. Make sure your implementation feels manageable, because when you begin to feel overwhelmed, the work becomes unsustainable and UDL will become another to-do on the endless list of teacher responsibilities.

Drinking the Water Is Not an Option

My seventh-grade art class was focused on demonstrating one or more watercolor techniques by applying their newly developed painting skills to a self-selected piece. I was not surprised to see one of my more rigid students catatonically staring at his paper covered in deep brown blotches. I approached him and gently asked, "What do you need to do?" "Put the brush in the water," he remarked. "Okay," I replied and glanced at his cup, which was empty. "Where is your water?" "I drank it." He replied dryly. "Were you thirsty?" "Not anymore."

Obviously drinking dirty paint water was not one of the options for the lesson. UDL does not mean you need to constantly outline basic expectations to ensure students do not present unexpected behaviors. Regardless of whether my lesson was universally designed, the student probably would have drunk the water, but because most of the class was engaged and learning, I was able to support one of the few disengaged students.

UDL allows me the instructional flexibility to address students' needs because more students are naturally invested in the art-making process. As issues and barriers arise during a lesson I can proactively respond, and in this case, reteach how to ask for water if you are thirsty.

Mistaken Names

Approximately 400 students a week walk into my art classroom. A month into the school year I typically know everyone's names, but I sometimes mismatch a student's name with another student who shares a similar physical appearance. These name identification errors persist with a few pupils throughout the year.

In December we were approaching our school-wide art show in which one of the goals was to have every single student present a piece they selected from their portfolio. In the fifth grade, there was a very reluctant artist whom I'd mistaken for one of my prolific and enthusiastic fourth-grade artists. Without realizing it, I talked to the fifth grader as if he were the fourth grader. At first, he seemed surprised by my encouraging and excited comments regarding his work in the art show; in retrospect, I realize why. He, however, responded so well to the explicit and direct praise that from that point forward he willingly engaged in art class and would ardently show me his pieces. He was also suddenly inspired not only to select a piece from his portfolio but to improve it.

The following day I had the fourth-grade class and realized I had shared the "wrong" feedback with the fifth grader. While my lapse in student names was a mistake, I realized that not providing explicit and positive comments to all students was an even greater mistake. My grudging fifth grader identified as an artist once I gave him effusive feedback. Lesson learned: focusing on the positive makes an impressionable impact and increases engagement in art even if my comments, in this case, were misplaced.

To Trace or Not to Trace?

The goal of a fourth-grade lesson was to create various cartoon bodies. Students had exposure to numerous options for representation and engagement. Forms of expression included using basic shapes to draw a figure, freehand draw, and/or use pre-cut shapes to structure a form.

Halfway through the independent work session, I noticed a student holding his paper up to the board where I was projecting images for ideas. He was trying to trace one of the forms, as the visual image from the projection was revealed on his paper. I thought, "That is such a practical way to meet the goal. This could be an option."

I privately lauded the student for his resourceful actions and enabled his tracing by providing him with painter's tape so he could affix his paper to the board. By the end of the period, three other students were tracing, but the remainder of the class seemed satisfied with their choices for expression.

The following week, however, most of the class wanted to trace directly from the LCD projection. While I noted that this could be one option, the end goal of the unit was to create a unique cartoon. I did not want students tracing long term. Pedagogically I felt it diminished creativity and represented only a basic skill, yet the previous week I had said yes.

With their increased demand for tracing, I regretted my decision as art class became a tracing class. The next two months of art classes with the fourth-grade always began with a discussion about why we were slowly going to stop tracing—that this temporary choice was just a means to scaffold their learning, but that the goal was to become independently skilled at drawing.

I eventually put a hard stop to tracing, but I wish I had originally said no. Students in this cohort were more fixated on perfection, and art was no longer a place to make mistakes. The tracing option also resulted in superfluous classroom management; everyone had to have at least one turn tracing from the LCD, and someone had to mediate the list of students who had not yet gone or who felt they did not get enough time. In retrospect, I realized that adding tracing as an option without preplanning deviated from the lesson's goal. Spontaneous decisions occur every day in teaching, but this one wasn't working.

I also learned that it is okay to say no sometimes. All options for expression, engagement, or representation are not always the best or most relevant means of achieving a goal. Your content can be just as accessible and barrier-free without always saying yes to a student request.

Implementing UDL will improve your instructional practice and student learning outcomes. UDL, however, does not mean your classroom will always be a barrier-free utopia. Professional growth takes time and requires risk taking. Implementing UDL will challenge your professional learning edge. This can sometimes result in failed lessons or missed opportunities for teachable moments. Critical reflection upon our failures, however, can inform future planning and lead to greater growth.

> **PAUSE AND THINK**
>
> 1. What experiences have you had in which a well-planned lesson did not meet the needs of all learners?
> 2. What were you able to learn from that experience?

Making UDL Implementation Sustainable

The boundless possibilities of UDL can be daunting, and any professional change can cause some discomfort. If you are finding that UDL seems challenging to implement, try to determine the specific barriers you are facing. One way to self-check your mindset and readiness to implement UDL into your classroom is to consider how you are feeling and work backward from there to name the category you are missing. For example, I resisted UDL in the earliest days of my career because I didn't see any incentive in implementing it. Years later, I felt anxiety and frustration as I grappled with a lack of skills and resources. Being able to name your own barriers in UDL implementation can help unravel what you need to be successful.

Another way to evaluate your needs for UDL implementation is to consider your personal will, skill, knowledge, capacity, and emotional intelligence (Aguilar, 2013). If you are experiencing barriers to actualizing UDL, check yourself with these questions:

- **Will:** Do you have the desire to apply UDL to your visual art curriculum and environment?
- **Skill:** Are you able to apply UDL to your visual art curriculum and environment?
- **Knowledge:** Do you have a basic understanding of the theory of UDL and how it may be applied?
- **Capacity:** Do you have the internal supports, time, and resources to implement UDL?
- **Emotional intelligence:** Are you able to recognize emotional reactions in others, and are you able to manage and express your own emotions productively?

One of the common reactions to UDL is: "I don't have time for this." While teachers do have limited time, UDL will eventually result in increasing your instructional and planning time. Initially, changes feel uncomfortable and may consume more time; however with practice, your students will be more engaged and have greater learning outcomes. The time you spend on reinforcing appropriate behavior will diminish as students gain self-regulation skills. The time you spend repeating the objective or steps to a project will dwindle when you have multiple means of representation. And finally, the barriers to expressing art will become less prevalent when students have options for demonstrating mastery of the goal.

If your will, skill, knowledge, capacity, or emotional intelligence continues to be a barrier to applying UDL, then start by exercising UDL on a smaller scale. Consider focusing lessons on one of the three principles or just one of the guidelines. You could also consider making one section of your lesson more UDL. Deliberately planning with the UDL framework, even on a small scale, is better than not using it at all.

> **SMART TIP**   You don't know what you don't know. Invite a peer or administrator to observe you using Novak and Rodriguez's UDL Progression Rubric (http://castpublishing.org/skinny-books/art-for-all/resources/), then ask for feedback on where your practice demonstrates UDL implementation and where you can grow. Or ask students to do it. They give the most authentic feedback!

A Word about Cell Phones

When the first edition of this book was published in 2018, I still owned a flip phone. Yes, I was that person who had to ask a friend to get an Uber because I didn't have the app, and I always carried cash because I couldn't Venmo. But the reality in my classroom was that 99% of my students had some form of a smartphone, and their phones were often a distraction during class. My flip phone was a running joke, but I was able to use it as a reason for students to put away their phones since I didn't have one.

This actually worked pretty well, but then my daughter was born, and I knew I'd want to capture lots of photos. A flip phone is full of barriers when it comes to taking a picture, so I upgraded to my first ever iPhone and instead of having a baby shower, I had a "Farewell Flip Phone Party." Now I couldn't use my flip phone as a reason for my class to put away their phones, even though my phone was and is always out of sight. Then the pandemic happened, and upon our return to in-person instruction, non-academic use of smartphones dramatically increased and caused intense distractions.

My school also doesn't have a school-wide no-phone policy. Each grade level approaches phone use differently, and I adapt to the policies of each cohort. My personal and pedagogical challenge is that I believe students in K–8 should not be using cell phones during class or even have them in their pockets, as phones are a distraction even when in a pocket (Haidt, 2024).

When a middle school student requests to use a phone to look up information or a video directly related to their project, I allow them to use the phone only after previewing what they are using it for, but I let them know if they or I see that the phone is a distraction and not being used for academic reasons, it will no longer be allowed. Sure enough, 95% of the time, the student is distracted within minutes. For the few 5% of students who have the willpower not to open another tab or app, they can continue to use their phone, and often it quickly gets put away because they got the information they needed and are back to art making.

Technology can have a place in the art room, but personal cell phone use is more often than not an "experience blocker" (Haidt, 2023). Countless studies have demonstrated that cell phone use among children and adolescents leads to increased anxiety and depression. They act as barriers to face-to-face socialization (Daly, 2023). They contribute to lower student achievement and reinforce a culture of inattention; "because of our phones, we are forever elsewhere" (Turkle, 2015).

Jonathan Haidt (2023) has said it succinctly: "No one is in support of a childhood with cell phones." School districts, educational programs, and whole countries that have banned cell phone use have seen dramatically positive results in both academic performance and emotional well-being (Buck, 2024).

So, with an inconsistent cell phone policy and a post-pandemic era of increased cell phone use, my instruction is faced with the biggest barrier yet. My greatest challenge with cell phone use has been with my middle school classes, especially my seventh-grade cohorts, who have art immediately after recess, a time when they are allowed to use their phones freely. Students come to class actively watching Netflix or playing video games, and simply telling them to put their devices away is completely ineffective and using my flip phone joke is irrelevant.

With my UDL mindset, I focus on the phone being the barrier, not the students. My goal is that students don't use their phones, and I approach this goal using five UDL related tactics:

- Storify the classroom policy
- Explain brain science
- Be compassionate
- Challenge students
- Ask for a chance

Zarretta Hammond (2015) notes one of the ways to implement Culturally Sustaining Pedagogy is by storifying your lessons. To hook my students into our discussion on cell phone use, I take them back in a time machine to the 1990s. I histrionically tell them that when we are in the art room, we are going to commit to a 1990 cell phone policy, which means their cell phones don't exist! I warm-heartedly explain that when I was in middle school, I had it much easier than them because I didn't have a device in my pocket that could show me anything I wanted at any time. I mime picking up a phone connected to a classroom wall as I describe how phones in the 90s were stationary. I playfully explain that sometimes the phone had a long spiral cord you could fidget with, or maybe it was even cordless, but you typically couldn't leave the room, or the call would be dropped. Plus, back in the 90s, phones were only phones! We couldn't do anything else with them, and most people didn't even have caller ID. When we wanted to call someone and we didn't know their phone number, do you know what we had to do?! We used this giant yellow directory called the phone book. It had tissue-paper-thin pages and 75 people with the last name Smith. Students are genuinely enthralled if you get into telling this story, and if you are a Gen Z teacher, you can lament missing out on a 90s childhood. I now complement the story with slide images of old phones, sitcom stars from the 90s using phones, and images of the phone book. I've had a student thoughtfully say, "Well, if we are in the 90s, I'm not born yet, so I can do whatever I want?!" It's a good point, so I reemphasize that the goal of our time travel only has to do with cell phone use.

Then I segue into brain science, since simply telling them the story isn't enough. We talk about attention span, distractibility, and how the phone can impact their focus. I share research on how each video, like, and swipe provides a hit of dopamine, while excessive cell phone use is linked to depression and anxiety. Usually, someone is using their phone by this point in the conversation. Instead of being punitive, it becomes a point proven, that it's hard to teach our brains to be present and disconnected from our devices.

I then focus on being compassionate, letting them know that their childhoods are much more challenging than mine was for many reasons, one of which is that they have to learn to live with cell phones and easy access to endless distractions. I let my students know I respect them and acknowledge that escaping the burden of their phones will not be easy. This is where the challenge comes in. I tell them I know they are strong and can do this, and I know there will be slip-ups, but I believe they can start to reprogram their brains, grow artistically, and not use their phone during class.

Finally, I wrap it up with a request. As not all students have bought in, I simply ask for a chance: just get into the art making without looking at or engaging with your phone. If you've never gone 20 minutes without it, try it and see what it is like. You've got nothing to lose.

Burnett et al. (2023) artfully put my classroom goal into perspective: "We must flip the script on teachers' perennial complaint. Instead of fretting that students' flagging attention doesn't serve education, we must make attention itself the thing being taught... What democracy most needs now is an attentive citizenry—human beings capable of looking up from their screens together."

To flip this script, approach the phone, not the student, as the barrier (Paul, 2023). My five-step approach to reducing phone use might not be as effective in your classroom depending on your demographic's relationships with their cell phones and your personal teaching style. Furthermore, I know there is a lot more I can do, and the school and district can do to more universally direct students' attention away from their screens (Daly, 2023; Haidt, 2024).

My experience in designing strategies to reduce cell phone use in the classroom has provided valuable insights that extend far beyond this specific challenge. The approaches I've developed are versatile and applicable to various barriers educators may face in the future. Storyfying a lesson, explaining brain science, being compassionate, challenging students, and asking for a chance are general approaches that will likely reduce future instructional challenges long after the cell phone is no longer my biggest barrier.

A Final Note

The role of the art teacher in schools is to inspire and train students to create. But beyond the obvious, we are also advocates, unifiers, validators, and barrier breakers. The arts bridge content areas. They reconceptualize the world and reinterpret it. Now your instruction needs to be reconceptualized and reframed to create accessible art instruction for all students.

This book shows my professional experience and knowledge, which will not be the same as yours. I'm still learning as an artist, as a teaching professional, and as a member of my school's team. As I teach, I glean more about the process of learning and the implementation of UDL every day. Parallel to this, each time I have the privilege of instructing other educators about UDL, I learn from their knowledge, expertise, and experiences. One of the most powerful methods for growing your UDL practice is by collaborating and communicating with colleagues you respect and trust. Observing others teach and being observed in non-evaluative settings can lead to powerful professional growth. Comprehending the three principles can seem seductively simple. Implementing them is the greater challenge and one that does not need to be approached alone.

Maya Angelou summed up how to sustainably approach UDL implementation in the visual art classroom in these eloquent words: "Do the best you can until you know better. When you know better, do better" (cited in Winfrey, 2014). Having read this book, hopefully, you "know better," and you feel inspired and eager to implement UDL into your visual art content and environment with enduring commitment to your students, passion for education, and love of learning.

Key Takeaways

- UDL in the visual arts will challenge you, bring mishaps and joy, and increase creative opportunities in your classroom.

- UDL takes time, and your teaching practice will continually grow; there isn't a neat bookend to UDL.

- Implementing UDL is an art form in itself. Take incremental steps, reflect on your work, and be open to new approaches to teaching and learning that share your love of art.

References

Aguilar, E. (2013, October 21). A coaching framework for thinking before acting. *Education Week Teacher Blogs*. http://blogs.edweek.org/teachers/coaching_teachers/2013/10/a_coaching_framework_for_think.html

American Psychological Association (2023). Later school start times promote adolescent well-being. https://www.apa.org/topics/children/school-start-times

Boisrond, C. (2017). If your teachers look like you, you may do better in school. NPR. https://www.npr.org/sections/ed/2017/09/29/552929074/if-your-teacher-looks-likes-you-you-may-do-better-in-school

Buck, D. (2024, May 9). The evidence for phone bans mounts. Education Gadfly. https://fordhaminstitute.org/national/commentary/evidence-phone-bans-mounts

Burnett, G., Loh, A., & Schmidt, P. (2023, November 27). Fight the powerful forces stealing our attention. *New York Times*.

California Department of Education. (2023, March 9). Culturally Sustaining Pedagogy. https://www.cde.ca.gov/pd/ee/culturallysustainingped.asp

CAST. (2024). *Universal Design for Learning Guidelines*. Version 3.0. Author.

CESE NSW What Works Best in Practice. (2023). A teacher's prompt guide to ChatGPT aligned with 'What works best.' https://stephenslighthouse.com/wp-content/uploads/2023/01/A-Teachers-Prompt-Guide-to-ChatGPT-aligned-with-What-Works-Best.pdf

Chajed, A. (2024). Culturally Sustaining Pedagogy: An introduction. The Center for Professional Education. Teachers College, Columbia University. https://cpet.tc.columbia.edu/news-press/culturally-sustaining-pedagogy-an-introduction

Chapman, G. D. (2010). *The 5 love languages: The secret to love that lasts*. Northfield Publishing.

Daly, T. (2023, December 8). Should schools ban cell phones? Education Gadfly. https://fordhaminstitute.org/national/commentary/should-schools-ban-cellphones

Douglas, K. & Jaquith, D. (2009). *Engaging learners through art-making, choice-based art education in the classroom*. Teachers College Press.

Dweck, C. S. (2006). *Mindset: The new psychology of success*. Random House.

Egalite, A. & Kisida, B. (2017). The effects of teacher match on students' academic perceptions and attitudes. *Educational Evaluation and Policy Analysis, 8*(1).

Gershenson, S., et al. (2017). The long-run impacts of same-race teachers. IZA Institute of Labor Economics. No. 10630.

Goodman, N. (1976). *Languages of art*. Hackett Publishing Company.

Haidt, J. (2023). Smartphones vs. smart kids: Heading off disaster in teen mental health. ExcelinEd National Summit in Education. https://www.youtube.com/watch?v=yVq4ARIlNVg

Haidt, J. (2024). *The anxious generation: How the great rewiring of childhood is causing an epidemic of mental illness*. Penguin Press.

Hammond, Z. (2015). *Culturally responsive teaching and the brain: Promoting authentic engagement and rigor among culturally and linguistically diverse students*. Corwin Press.

Heissel, J., & Norris, S. (2019). Rise and shine: how school start times affect academic performance. *Education Next, 19*(3), 54–61.

Hetland, L., Winner, E., Veenema S., & Sheridan, K. M. (2013). *Studio thinking 2: The real benefits of visual arts education*. Teachers College Press.

Hughes, C. (2024). *The end of race politics: Arguments for a colorblind America*. Penguin.

Institute of Education Sciences, Regional Educational Laboratory Pacific. (2024). What is Culturally Sustaining Pedagogy? https://ies.ed.gov/ncee/rel/regions/pacific/pdf/REL_CulturallySustainingPedagogy_508.pdf

Lee, R. (2015, August 31). What's missing from the conversation: the growth mindset in cultural competency. National Association of Independent Schools. https://www.nais.org/learn/independent-ideas/august-2015/what%E2%80%99s-missing-from-the-conversation-the-growth-m/

Lindsay, C. A., & Hart, C. M. D. (2017). Exposure to same-race teachers and student disciplinary outcomes for black students in North Carolina. *Educational Evaluation and Policy Analysis, 39*(3), 485–510. https://doi.org/10.3102/0162373717693109

Meyer, A., Rose, D. H., & Gordon, D. (2014). Universal design for learning: Theory and practice. CAST Professional Publishing.

Novak, K. & Rodriguez, K. (2018). UDL progression rubric. http://castpublishing.org/novak-rodriguez-udl-progression-rubric

Paul, P. (2023, November 20). Kids aren't the ones with the cellphone problem. *New York Times*.

Paulmann, S. & Weinstein, N. (2023). Teachers' motivational prosody: A pre-registered experimental test of children's reactions to tone of voice used by teachers. *British Journal of Educational Psychology, 93*(2). https://doi.org/10.1111/bjep.12567

Philips, L. (2013, January 22). Top 10 skills children learn from the arts. *Washington Post*. https://www.washingtonpost.com/news/answer-sheet/wp/2013/01/22/top-10-skills-children-learn-from-the-arts/?utm_term=.7bebd0337fa9

Project Implicit (March 2024). https://www.projectimplicit.net/

Roose, K. (2023, March 30). How should I use A.I. chatbots like ChatGPT? *New York Times*.

Smooth, J. (2011, November 15). How I learned to stop worrying and love discussing race. TEDx Hampshire College.

Starck, J., Riddle, T., Sinclair, S., & Warikoo, N. (2020). Teachers are people too: Examining the racial bias of teachers compared to other American adults. *Educational Researcher, 49*(4).

Turkel, S. (2015). *Reclaiming conversation: The power of talk in a digital age*. Penguin.

Vinopal, K. & Holt, S. (2019). Rookie mistakes: the interplay of teacher experience and racial representation. *Educational Researcher, 48*(7).

Winfrey, O. (2014). *What I know for sure*. Flatiron Books.

Additional Reading

Baldwin, J. (1962, November 29). *The artist's struggle for integrity.* Speech presented in New York City's Community Church, New York City, https://soundcloud.com/brainpicker/james-baldwin-the-artists-struggle-for-integrity-full-lecture

Baker, J. A., Grant, S., & Morlock, L. (2008). The teacher-student relationship as a developmental context for children with internalizing or externalizing behavior problems. *School Psychology Quarterly, 23*(1), 3–15.

CAST. (2018). *Universal Design for Learning Guidelines.* Version 2.2. Author.

Cooper, K., Kintz, T., & Miness, A. (2016). Reflectiveness, adaptivity, and support: How teacher agency promotes student engagement. *American Journal of Education 123*(1), 109–136.

Davis, J. H. (2005). *Framing education as art: The octopus has a good day.* Teachers College Press.

Davis, J. H. (2008). *Why our schools need the arts.* Teachers College Press.

Deans for Impact (2015). *The science of learning.* Author.

Dotterer, A.M., & Lowe, K. (2011). Classroom context, school engagement, and academic achievement and early adolescence. *Journal of Youth Adolescence, 40,* 1649–1660. doi:10.1007/210964-011-9647-5.

Dweck, C. S. (2016, January 13). What having a "growth mindset" actually means. *Harvard Business Review* blog. https://hbr.org/2016/01/what-having-a-growth-mindset-actually-means#comment-section

Eisner, E. (2002). *What the arts teach and how it shows*. Yale University Press.

Fredricks, J., McColskey, W., Meli, J., Mordica, J., Montrosse, B., & Mooney, K. (2011). Measuring student engagement in upper elementary through high school: a description of 21 instruments. (Issues & Answers Report, REL 2011–No. 098). Washington, DC: U.S. Department of Education, Institute of Education Sciences, National Center for Education Evaluation and Regional Assistance, Regional Educational Laboratory Southeast. http://ies.ed.gov/ncee/edlabs

Fredrickson, B. L., & Branigan, C. (2005). Positive emotions broaden the scope of attention and thought-action repertoires. *Cognition and Emotion, 19*(3), 313–332.

Gardner, H. (1973). *The arts and human development: A psychological study of the artistic process*. John Wiley & Sons.

Gardner, H. (1982). *Art, mind, and brain: A cognitive approach to creativity*. Basic Books, Inc.

Gardner, H., & Winner, E. (1982). First intimations of artistry. In S. Strauss (Ed.), *U-shaped behavioral growth* (pp.147–167). Academic Press.

Giangreco, M. (2003). Moving toward inclusive education. In W. L. Heward (Ed.), *Exceptional children: An introduction to special education* (7th ed.) (pp. 78–79). Englewood Cliffs, NJ: Merrill.

Glass, D., Blair, K., & Ganley, P. (2012). Universal Design for Learning and the arts option. In T. E. Hall, A. Meyer, & D. H. Rose (Eds.), *Universal Design for Learning in the classroom: Practical applications* (pp. 106–119). Guilford Press.

Glass, D., Meyer, A., & Rose, D. H. (Spring 2013). Universal Design for Learning and the arts. In *Harvard Educational Review 83*(1) 98–120.

Hall, T., Meyer, A., & Rose, D. H. (Eds.). (2012). *Universal Design for Learning in the classroom: Practical applications*. Guilford Press.

Hetland L., & Winner E. (2001). The arts and academic achievement: What the evidence shows. In *Arts Education Policy Review 102*(5) 3–6. Taylor & Francis Group.

Hippocrates (n.d.). *Oath of Hippocrates*. In *Harvard Classics*, Vol 38. P.F. Collier and Son, 1910.

Immordino-Yang, M., & Damasio, A. (2007). We feel, therefore we learn: The relevance of affective and social neuroscience to education. *Mind, Brain, and Education, 1*(1), 3–10.

Knoster, T. (1991, June). Factors in managing complex change. Material presentation at TASH conference, Washington, DC. Association for People with Severe Disabilities.

Lawson, M., & Lawson, H. (2013). New conceptual frameworks for student engagement research, policy, and practice. *Review of Educational Research, 83*(3), 432–79.

Nathan, L. (2012, February). All students are artists. *Educational Leadership, 69*(5) 48–51.

National Coalition of Core Arts Standards (n.d.). National Core Arts Standards: A conceptual framework for arts learning. Retrieved June 28, 2017, from nccas.wikispaces.com/Conceptual+Framework

National Core Arts Standards (2014). State Education Agency Directors of Arts Education (SEADAE) on behalf of NCCAS. Retrieved June 1, 2017, from www.nationalartsstandards.org

Nehring, J., Charner-Laird M., & Szczesiul S. (2017). What real high performance looks like. *Phi Delta Kappan, 78*(7) 38–42.

Nelson, L. L. (2013). *Design and deliver: Planning and teaching using Universal Design for Learning*. Brookes Publishing.

Novak, K. (2014). *UDL Now!* CAST Professional Publishing.

Philips, L. (2013, January 29). Why we love artists but not art education. *Washington Post*. https://www.washingtonpost.com/news/answer-sheet/wp/2013/01/29/why-we-love-artists-but-not-arts-education/?utm_term=.3ea170904f75

Picasso, P. (n.d.). BrainyQuote.com. https://www.brainyquote.com/quotes/quotes/p/pablopicas104106.html

Salend, S., & Whittaker, C. (2017). UDL: A blueprint for learning success. *Educational Leadership, 74*(7), 59–63.

Schmoker, M. (2004). Tipping point: From feckless reform to substantive instructional improvement. *Phi Delta Kappan, 85*(6), 424–438.

Storbeck, J., & Clore, G. L. (2012). On the interdependence of cognition and emotion. In Rappolt-Schlichtmann, G., Daley, S.G., & Rose, L.T. (Eds), *A research reader in universal design for learning* (pp. 62–89). Harvard Education Press.

U.S. Department of Education, Institute of Education Sciences, National Center for Education Statistics, National Assessment of Educational Progress (NAEP) (2016). *2016 National assessment of educational progress at grade 8: Music and visual arts*. https://www.nationsreportcard.gov/arts_2016/

Whitted, K.S. (2011). Understanding how social and emotional skill deficits contribute to school failure. *Preventing School Failure, 55*(1), 10–16.

Winner, E., & Hetland, L. (2007). Art for our sake. *Arts Education Policy Review, 109*(5), 29–32.

Yazzie-Mintz, E. (2010). Leading for engagement. In *Principal Leadership, 10*(7), 54–58.

Yenawine, P. (2013). *Visual thinking strategies: Using art to deepen learning across school disciplines*. Harvard Education Press.

CAST Skinny Books®

"Don't tell me everything. Just give me the skinny!"™

CAST Professional Publishing produces books that help educators at all levels improve their practice—and change students' lives—through Universal Design for Learning (UDL). We create, nurture, and distribute exceptional media products that inspire and inform educational research, instructional practice, and policy making for the betterment of all.

Skinny Books by CAST address critical topics of education practice through brief, informative publications that emphasize practical tips and strategies. We talk about these books as "multivitamins"—densely packed with helpful knowledge in a small, digestible format.

We welcome new proposals. Got an idea? Let us know at *publishing@cast.org*.

While every Skinny Book will be in tune with the inclusive principles of Universal Design for Learning, not every title needs to address UDL specifically. For those that do, the authors may assume readers have a knowledge of UDL already, as we've done in *Art for All*.

If you need an introduction to UDL, visit *udlguidelines.cast.org*.

You can also purchase this or many other titles on UDL from *www.castpublishing.org*.

MORE FROM ⊙ CAST

CAST is a nonprofit education research and development organization that created the Universal Design for Learning framework and UDL Guidelines. Our mission is to transform education design and practice until learning has no limits.

CAST supports learners and educators at every level through a variety of offerings:

- Innovative professional development
- Accessibility and inclusive technology resources
- Research, design, and development of inclusive and effective solutions
- Credentials for Universal Design for Learning
- And much more

Visit *www.cast.org* to learn more.